AWARENESS

AWARENESS

*A de Mello Spirituality Conference
in His Own Words*

ANTHONY DE MELLO, S.J.
Edited by J. Francis Stroud, S.J.

IMAGE BOOKS

DOUBLEDAY

NEW YORK LONDON TORONTO SYDNEY AUCKLAND

An Image Book
PUBLISHED BY DOUBLEDAY
a division of Bantam Doubleday Dell Publishing Group, Inc.
1540 Broadway, New York, New York 10036

IMAGE, DOUBLEDAY, and the portrayal of a deer drinking
from a stream are trademarks of Doubleday, a division of
Bantam Doubleday Dell Publishing Group, Inc.

This Image Books edition published May 1992 by special
arrangement with Doubleday.

Library of Congress Cataloging-in-Publication Data

De Mello, Anthony, 1931–1987
    Awareness : a de Mello spirituality conference in his
own words / Anthony de Mello : edited by J. Francis
Stroud.
        p.   cm.
    1. Spiritual life—Catholic authors.   I. Stroud, J.
Francis. II. Title.
    [BX2350.2.D446   1992]
    248.4′82—dc20   91-37433
                                                     CIP

ISBN 0-385-24937-3

30 29 28 27 26 25 24 23

CONTENTS

AWARENESS

FOREWORD

Tony de Mello on an occasion among friends was asked to say a few words about the nature of his work. He stood up, told a story which he repeated later in conferences, and which you will recognize from his book *Song of the Bird*. To my astonishment, he said this story applied to me.

> A man found an eagle's egg and put it in a nest of a barnyard hen. The eaglet hatched with the brood of chicks and gew up with them.
>
> All his life the eagle did what the barnyard chicks did, thinking he was a barnyard chicken. He scratched the earth for worms and insects. He clucked and cackled. And he would thrash his wings and fly a few feet into the air.
>
> Years passed and the eagle grew very old. One day he saw a magnicifent bird above him in the cloudless sky. It glided in graceful majesty among the powerful wind currents, with scarcely a beat of its strong golden wings.
>
> The old eagle looked up in awe. "Who's that?" he asked.
>
> "That's the eagle, the king of the birds," said his neighbor. "He belongs to the sky. We belong to the earth—we're chickens." So the eagle lived and died a chicken, for that's what he thought he was.

Astonished? At first I felt downright insulted! Was he publicly likening me to a barnyard chicken? In a sense, yes, and also, no. Insulting? Never. That wasn't Tony's way. But he was telling me and these people that in his eyes I was a "golden eagle," unaware of the heights to which I could soar. This story made me understand the measure of the man, his genuine love and respect for people while always telling the truth. That was what his work was all about, waking people up to the reality of their greatness. This was Tony de Mello at his best, proclaiming the message of "awareness," seeing the light we are to ourselves and to others, recognizing we are better than we know.

This book captures Tony in flight, doing just that—in live dialogue and interaction—touching on all the themes that enliven the hearts of those who listen.

Maintaining the spirit of his live words, and sustaining his spontaneity with a responsive audience on the printed page was the task I faced after his death. Thanks to the wonderful support I enjoyed from George McCauley, S.J., Joan Brady, John Culkin, and others too numerous to single out, the exciting, entertaining, provocative hours Tony spent communicating with real people have been wonderfully captured in the pages that follow.

Enjoy the book. Let the words slip into your soul and listen, as Tony would suggest, with your heart. Hear his stories, and you'll hear your own. Let me leave you alone with Tony—a spiritual guide—a friend you will have for life.

—J. Francis Stroud, S.J.
De Mello Spirituality Center
Fordham University
Bronx, New York

ON _WAKING_ UP

Spirituality means waking up. Most people, even though they don't know it, are asleep. They're born asleep, they live asleep, they marry in their sleep, they breed children in their sleep, they die in their sleep without ever waking up. They never understand the loveliness and the beauty of this thing that we call human existence. You know, all mystics —Catholic, Christian, non-Christian, no matter what their theology, no matter what their religion—are unanimous on one thing: that all is well, all is well. Though everything is a mess, all is well. Strange paradox, to be sure. But, tragically, most people never get to see that all is well because they are asleep. They are having a nightmare.

Last year on Spanish television I heard a story about this gentleman who knocks on his son's door. "Jaime," he says, "wake up!" Jaime answers, "I don't want to get up, Papa." The father shouts, "Get up, you have to go to school." Jaime says, "I don't want to go to school." "Why not?" asks the father. "Three reasons," says Jaime. "First, because it's so dull; second, the kids tease me; and third, I hate school." And the father says, "Well, I am going to give you three reasons why you _must_ go to school. First, because it is your duty; second, because you are forty-five years old, and third, because you are the headmaster." Wake up, wake up! You've grown up. You're too big to be asleep. Wake up! Stop playing with your toys.

Most people tell you they want to get out of kindergarten, but don't believe them. Don't believe them! All they want you to do is to mend their broken toys. "Give me back my wife. Give me back my job. Give me back my money. Give me back my reputation, my success." This is what they want; they want their toys replaced. That's all. Even the best psychologist will tell you that, that people don't really want to be cured. What they want is relief; a cure is painful.

Waking up is unpleasant, you know. You are nice and comfortable in bed. It's irritating to be woken up. That's the reason the wise guru will not attempt to wake people up. I hope I'm going to be wise here and make no attempt whatsoever to wake you up if you are asleep. It is really none of my business, even though I say to you at times, "Wake up!" My business is to do my thing, to dance my dance. If you profit from it, fine; if you don't, too bad! As the Arabs say, "The nature of rain is the same, but it makes thorns grow in the marshes and flowers in the gardens."

WILL I BE OF HELP TO YOU IN THIS RETREAT?

Do you think I am going to help anybody? No! Oh, no, no, no, no, no! Don't expect me to be of help to anyone. Nor do I expect to damage anyone. If you are damaged, you did it; and if you are helped, you did it. You really did! You think people help you? They don't. You think people support you? They don't.

There was a woman in a therapy group I was conducting

once. She was a religious sister. She said to me, "I don't feel supported by my superior." So I said, "What do you mean by that?" And she said, "Well, my superior, the provincial superior, never shows up at the novitiate where I am in charge, never. She never says a word of appreciation." I said to her, "All right, let's do a little role playing. Pretend I know your provincial superior. In fact, pretend I know exactly what she thinks about you. So I say to you (acting the part of the provincial superior), 'You know, Mary, the reason I don't come to that place you're in is because it is the one place in the province that is trouble-free—no problems. I know you're in charge, so all is well.' How do you feel now?" She said, "I feel great." Then I said to her, "All right, would you mind leaving the room for a minute or two. This is part of the exercise." So she did. While she was away, I said to the others in the therapy group, "I am still the provincial superior, O.K.? Mary out there is the worst novice director I have ever had in the whole history of the province. In fact, the reason I don't go to the novitiate is because I can't bear to see what she is up to. It's simply awful. But if I tell her the truth, it's only going to make those novices suffer all the more. We are getting somebody to take her place in a year or two; we are training someone. In the meantime I thought I would say those nice things to her to keep her going. What do you think of that?" They answered, "Well, it was really the only thing you could do under the circumstances." Then I brought Mary back into the group and asked her if she still felt great. "Oh yes," she said. Poor Mary! She thought she was being supported when she wasn't. The point is that most of what we feel and think we conjure up for ourselves in our heads, including this business of being helped by people.

Do you think you help people because you are in love with them? Well, I've got news for you. You are never in love with anyone. You're only in love with your prejudiced and hopeful idea of that person. Take a minute to think about that: You are never in love with anyone, you're in love with your prejudiced idea of that person. Isn't that how you fall out of love? Your idea changes, doesn't it? "How could you let me down when I trusted you so much?" you say to someone. Did you really trust them? You never trusted anyone. Come off it! That's part of society's brainwashing. You never trust anyone. You only trust your judgment about that person. So what are you complaining about? The fact is that you don't like to say, "My judgment was lousy." That's not very flattering to you, is it? So you prefer to say, "How could you have let me down?"

So there it is: People don't really want to grow up, people don't really want to change, people don't really want to be happy. As someone so wisely said to me, "Don't try to make them happy, you'll only get in trouble. Don't try to teach a pig to sing; it wastes your time and it irritates the pig." Like the businessman who goes into a bar, sits down, and sees this fellow with a banana in his ear—a banana in his ear! And he thinks, "I wonder if I should mention that to him. No, it's none of my business." But the thought nags at him. So after having a drink or two, he says to the fellow, "Excuse me, ah, you've got a banana in your ear." The fellow says, "What?" The businessman repeats, "You've got a banana in your ear." Again the fellow says, "What was that?" "You've got a banana in your ear!" the businessman shouts. "Talk louder," the fellow says, "I've got a banana in my ear!"

So it's useless. "Give up, give up, give up," I say to myself. Say your thing and get out of here. And if they profit, that's fine, and if they don't, too bad!

❦

ON THE PROPER KIND OF SELFISHNESS

The first thing I want you to understand, if you really want to wake up, is that you don't want to wake up. The first step to waking up is to be honest enough to admit to yourself that you don't like it. You don't want to be happy. Want a little test? Let's try it. It will take you exactly one minute. You could close your eyes while you're doing it or you could keep them open. It doesn't really matter. Think of someone you love very much, someone you're close to, someone who is precious to you, and say to that person in your mind, "I'd rather have happiness than have you." See what happens. "I'd rather be happy than have you. If I had a choice, no question about it, I'd choose happiness." How many of you felt selfish when you said this? Many, it seems. See how we've been brainwashed? See how we've been

brainwashed into thinking, "How could I be so selfish?"
But look at who's being selfish. Imagine somebody saying
to *you,* "How could you be so selfish that you'd choose
happiness over me?" Would you not feel like responding,
"Pardon me, but how could *you* be so selfish that *you* would
demand I choose you above my own happiness?!"

A woman once told me that when she was a child her
Jesuit cousin gave a retreat in the Jesuit church in Milwau-
kee. He opened each conference with the words: "The test
of love is sacrifice, and the gauge of love is unselfishness."
That's marvelous! I asked her, "Would you want me to love
you at the cost of my happiness?" "Yes," she answered. Isn't
that delightful? Wouldn't that be wonderful? *She* would
love me at the cost of *her* happiness and *I* would love *her* at
the cost of *my* happiness, and so you've got *two* unhappy
people, but *long live love!*

ON WANTING HAPPINESS

I was saying that we don't want to be happy. We want
other things. Or let's put it more accurately: We don't want
to be unconditionally happy. I'm ready to be happy *provided*
I have this and that and the other thing. But this is really to
say to our friend or to our God or to anyone, "You are my
happiness. *If I don't get you,* I refuse to be happy." It's so
important to understand that. We cannot imagine being
happy without those conditions. That's pretty accurate. We

cannot conceive of being happy without them. We've been taught to place our happiness in them.

So that's the first thing we need to do if we want to come awake, which is the same thing as saying: if we want to love, if we want freedom, if we want joy and peace and spirituality. In that sense, spirituality is the most practical thing in the whole wide world. I challenge anyone to think of anything more practical than spirituality as I have defined it—not piety, not devotion, not religion, not worship, but spirituality—waking up, waking up! Look at the heartache everywhere, look at the loneliness, look at the fear, the confusion, the conflict in the hearts of people, inner conflict, outer conflict. Suppose somebody gave you a way of getting rid of all of that? Suppose somebody gave you a way to stop that tremendous drainage of energy, of health, of emotion that comes from these conflicts and confusion. Would you want that? Suppose somebody showed us a way whereby we would truly love one another, and be at peace, be at love. Can you think of anything more practical than that? But, instead, you have people thinking that big business is more practical, that politics is more practical, that science is more practical. What's the earthly use of putting a man on the moon when *we* cannot live on the earth?

ARE WE TALKING ABOUT PSYCHOLOGY IN THIS SPIRITUALITY COURSE?

Is psychology more practical than spirituality? Nothing is more practical than spirituality. What can the poor psychologist do? He can only relieve the pressure. I'm a psychologist myself, and I practice psychotherapy, and I have this great conflict within me when I have to choose sometimes between psychology and spirituality. I wonder if that makes sense to anybody here. It didn't make sense to me for many years.

I'll explain. It didn't make sense to me for many years until I suddenly discovered that people have to suffer *enough* in a relationship so that they get disillusioned with *all* relationships. Isn't that a terrible thing to think? They've got to suffer *enough* in a relationship before they wake up and say, "I'm sick of it! There must be a better way of living than depending on another human being." And what was I doing as a psychotherapist? People were coming to me with their relationship problems, with their communication problems, etc., and sometimes what I did was a help. But sometimes, I'm sorry to say, it wasn't, because it kept people asleep. Maybe they should have suffered a little *more*. Maybe they ought to touch rock bottom and say, "I'm sick of it *all.*" It's only when you're sick of your sickness that you'll get out of it. Most people go to a psychiatrist or a psychologist to get relief. I repeat: to get relief. Not to get out of it.

There's the story of little Johnny who, they say, was

mentally retarded. But evidently he wasn't, as you'll learn from this story. Johnny goes to modeling class in his school for special children and he gets his piece of putty and he's modeling it. He takes a little lump of putty and goes to a corner of the room and he's playing with it. The teacher comes up to him and says, "Hi, Johnny." And Johnny says, "Hi." And the teacher says, "What's that you've got in your hand?" And Johnny says, "This is a lump of cow dung." The teacher asks, "What are you making out of it?" He says, "I'm making a teacher."

The teacher thought, "Little Johnny has regressed." So she calls out to the principal, who was passing by the door at that moment, and says, "Johnny has regressed."

So the principal goes up to Johnny and says, "Hi, son." And Johnny says, "Hi." And the principal says, "What do you have in your hand?" And he says, "A lump of cow dung." "What are you making out of it?" And he says, "A principal."

The principal thinks that this is a case for the school psychologist. "Send for the psychologist!"

The psychologist is a clever guy. He goes up and says, "Hi." And Johnny says, "Hi." And the psychologist says, "I know what you've got in your hand." "What?" "A lump of cow dung." Johnny says, "Right." "And I know what you're making out of it." "What?" "You're making a psychologist." "Wrong. Not enough cow dung!" And they called him mentally retarded!

The poor psychologists, they're doing a good job. They really are. There are times when psychotherapy is a tremen-

dous help, because when you're on the verge of going in-
sane, raving mad, you're about to become either a psychotic
or a mystic. That's what the mystic is, the opposite of the
lunatic. Do you know one sign that you've woken up? It's
when you are asking yourself, "Am I crazy, or are all of
them crazy?" It really is. Because we are crazy. The whole
world is crazy. Certifiable lunatics! The only reason we're
not locked up in an institution is that there are so many of
us. So we're crazy. We're living on crazy ideas about love,
about relationships, about happiness, about joy, about everything. We're crazy to the point, I've come to believe,
that if everybody agrees on something, you can be sure it's
wrong! Every new idea, every great idea, when it first
began was in a minority of one. That man called Jesus
Christ—minority of one. Everybody was saying something
different from what he was saying. The Buddha—minority
of one. Everybody was saying something different from
what he was saying. I think it was Bertrand Russell who
said, "Every great idea starts out as a blasphemy." That's
well and accurately put. You're going to hear lots of blas-
phemies during these days. "He hath blasphemed!" Because
people are crazy, they're lunatics, and the sooner you see
this, the better for your mental and spiritual health. Don't
trust them. Don't trust your best friends. Get disillusioned
with your best friends. They're very clever. As *you* are in
your dealings with everybody else, though you probably
don't know it. Ah, you're so wily, and subtle, and clever.
You're putting on a great act.

I'm not being very complimentary here, am I? But I

repeat: You want to wake up. You're putting on a great act. And you don't even know it. You think you're being so loving. Ha! Whom are you loving? Even your self-sacrifice gives you a good feeling, doesn't it? "I'm sacrificing myself! I'm living up to my ideal." But you're getting something out of it, aren't you? You're always getting something out of everything you do, until you wake up.

So there it is: step one. Realize that you don't want to wake up. It's pretty difficult to wake up when you have been hypnotized into thinking that a scrap of old newspaper is a check for a million dollars. How difficult it is to tear yourself away from that scrap of old newspaper.

— 2 "THAT YOU DON'T WANT TO BE HAPPY"
P. 19

NEITHER IS RENUNCIATION THE SOLUTION

Anytime you're practicing renunciation, you're deluded. How about *that!* You're deluded. What are you renouncing? Anytime you renounce something, you are tied forever to the thing you renounce. There's a guru in India who says, "Every time a prostitute comes to me, she's talking about nothing but God. She says I'm sick of this life that I'm living. I want God. But every time a priest comes to me he's talking about nothing but sex." Very well, when you renounce something, you're stuck to it forever. When you fight something, you're tied to it forever. As long as you're fighting it, you are giving it power. You give it as much power as you are using to fight it.

This includes communism and everything else. So you must "receive" your demons, because when you fight them, you empower them. Has nobody ever told you this? When you renounce something, you're tied to it. The only way to get out of this is to see through it. Don't renounce it, *see through it*. Understand its true value and you won't need to renounce it; it will just drop from your hands. But of course, if you don't see that, if you're hypnotized into thinking that you won't be happy without this, that, or the other thing, you're stuck. What we need to do for you is not what so-called spirituality attempts to do—namely, to get you to make sacrifices, to renounce things. That's useless. You're still asleep. What we need to do is to help you understand, understand, understand. If you understood, you'd simply drop the desire for it. This is another way of saying: If you woke up, you'd simply drop the desire for it.

☙
LISTEN AND UNLEARN

Some of us get woken up by the harsh realities of life. We suffer so much that we wake up. But people keep bumping again and again into life. They still go on sleepwalking. They never wake up. Tragically, it never occurs to them that there may be another way. It never occurs to them that there may be a better way. Still, if *you* haven't been bumped sufficiently by life, and you haven't suffered enough, then there is another way: to *listen*. I don't mean you have to agree with what I'm saying. That wouldn't be listening. Believe me, it really doesn't matter whether you agree with what I'm saying or you don't. Because agreement and disagreement have to do with words and concepts and theories. They don't have anything to do with truth. Truth is never expressed in words. Truth is sighted suddenly, as a result of a certain attitude. So you could be disagreeing with me and still sight the truth. But there has to be an attitude of openness, of willingness to discover something new. That's important, not your agreeing with me or disagreeing with me. After all, most of what I'm giving you is really theories. No theory adequately covers reality. So I can speak to you, not of the truth, but of obstacles to the truth. Those I can describe. I cannot describe the truth. No one can. All I can do is give you a description of your falsehoods, so that you can drop them. All I can do for you is challenge your beliefs and the belief system that makes you unhappy. All I can do for you is help you to unlearn. That's what learning is all about where spirituality is concerned: unlearning, unlearning almost everything you've been taught. A willingness to unlearn, to listen.

Are you listening, as most people do, in order to confirm what you already think? Observe your reactions as I talk. Frequently you'll be startled or shocked or scandalized or irritated or annoyed or frustrated. Or you'll be saying, "Great!"

But are you listening for what will confirm what you

already think? Or are you listening in order to discover something new? That is important. It is difficult for sleeping people. Jesus proclaimed the good news yet he was rejected. Not because it was good, but because it was new. We hate the new. We hate it! And the sooner we face up to that fact, the better. We don't want new things, particularly when they're disturbing, particularly when they involve change. Most particularly if it involves saying, "I was wrong." I remember meeting an eighty-seven-year-old Jesuit in Spain; he'd been my professor and rector in India thirty or forty years ago. And he attended a workshop like this. "I should have heard you speak sixty years ago," he said. "You know something. I've been wrong all my life." God, to listen to that! It's like looking at one of the wonders of the world. That, ladies and gentlemen, is *faith!* An openness to the truth, no matter what the consequences, no matter where it leads you and when you don't even know where it's going to lead you. That's faith. *Not* belief, but faith. Your beliefs give you a lot of security, but faith is insecurity. You don't know. You're ready to follow and you're open, you're wide open! You're ready to listen. And, mind you, being open does not mean being gullible, it doesn't mean swallowing whatever the speaker is saying. Oh no. You've got to challenge everything I'm saying. But challenge it from an attitude of openness, not from an attitude of stubbornness. And challenge it all. Recall those lovely words of Buddha when he said, "Monks and scholars must not accept my words out of respect, but must analyze them the way a goldsmith analyzes gold—by cutting, scraping, rubbing, melting."

When you do that, you're listening. You've taken another major step toward awakening. The first step, as I said, was a readiness to admit that you don't want to wake up, that you don't want to be happy. There are all kinds of resistances to that within you. The second step is a readiness to understand, to listen, to challenge your whole belief system. Not just your religious beliefs, your political beliefs, your social beliefs, your psychological beliefs, but all of them. A readiness to reappraise them all, in the Buddha's metaphor. And I'll give you plenty of opportunity to do that here.

THE MASQUERADE OF CHARITY

Charity is really self-interest masquerading under the form of altruism. You say that it is very difficult to accept that there may be times when you are not honest to goodness really trying to be loving or trustful. Let me simplify it. Let's make it as simple as possible. Let's even make it as blunt and extreme as possible, at least to begin with. There are two types of selfishness. The first type is the one where I give myself the pleasure of pleasing myself. That's what we generally call self-centeredness. The second is when I give myself the pleasure of pleasing others. That would be a more refined kind of selfishness.

The first one is very obvious, but the second one is hidden, very hidden, and for that reason more dangerous, because we get to feel that we're really great. But maybe we're not all that great after all. You protest when I say that. That's great!

You, madam, you say that, in your case, you live alone, and go to the rectory and give several hours of your time. But you also admit you're really doing it for a selfish reason —your need to be needed—and you also know you need to be needed in a way that makes you feel like you're contributing to the world a little bit. But you also claim that, because they also need you to do this, it's a two-way street.

You're almost enlightened! We've got to learn from you. That's right. She is saying, "I give something, I get something." She is right. I go out to help, I give something, I get something. That's beautiful. That's true. That's real. That isn't charity, that's enlightened self-interest.

And you, sir, you point out that the gospel of Jesus is ultimately a gospel of self-interest. We achieve eternal life by our acts of charity. "Come blest of my Father, when I was hungry, you gave me to eat," and so on. You say that perfectly confirms what I've said. When we look at Jesus, you say, we see that his acts of charity were acts of ultimate self-interest, to win souls for eternal life. And you see that as the whole thrust and meaning of life: the achievement of self-interest by acts of charity.

All right. But you see, you are cheating a bit because you brought religion into this. It's legitimate. It's valid. But how would it be if I deal with the gospels, with the Bible, with Jesus, toward the *end* of this retreat. I will say this much now to complicate it even more. "I was hungry, and you gave me to eat, I was thirsty and you gave me to drink," and what do they reply? "When? When did we do it? We didn't know it." They were unconscious! I sometimes have a horrid fantasy where the king says, "I was hungry and you gave me to eat," and the people on the right side say, "That's right, Lord, we *know*." "I wasn't talking to you," the king tells them. "It doesn't follow the script; you're not *supposed* to have known." Isn't that interesting? But *you* know. You know the inner pleasure you have while doing acts of charity. Aha! That's right! It's the opposite of someone who says, "What's so great about what I did? I did something, I got something. I had no notion I was doing anything good. My left hand had no idea what my right hand was doing." You know, a good is never so good as when you have no awareness that you're doing good. You are never so good as when you have no consciousness that you're good. Or as the great Sufi would say, "A saint is one until he or she knows it." Unselfconscious! Unselfconscious!

Some of you object to this. You say, "Isn't the pleasure I receive in giving, isn't that eternal life right here and now?" I wouldn't know. I call pleasure, pleasure, and nothing more. For the time being, at least until we get into religion later on. But I want you to understand something right at the beginning, that religion is not—I repeat: *not*—necessarily connected with spirituality. Please keep religion out of this for the time being.

All right, you ask, what about the soldier who falls on a

grenade to keep it from hurting others? And what about the man who got into a truck full of dynamite and drove into the American camp in Beirut? How about him? "Greater love than this no one has." But the Americans don't think so. He did it deliberately. He was terrible, wasn't he? But he wouldn't think so, I assure you. He thought he was going to heaven. That's right. Just like your soldier falling on the grenade.

I'm trying to get at a picture of an action where there is not self, where you're awake and what you do is done through you. Your deed in that case becomes a happening. "Let it be done to me." I'm not excluding that. But when *you* do it, I'm searching for the selfishness. Even if it is only "I'll be remembered as a great hero," or "I'd never be able to live if I didn't do this. I'd never be able to live with the thought if I ran away." But remember, I'm not excluding the other kind of act. I didn't say that there never is any act where there is not self. Maybe there is. We'll have to explore that. A mother saving a child—saving *her* child, you say. But how come she's not saving the neighbor's child? It's the *hers*. It's the soldier dying for *his* country. Many such deaths bother me. I ask myself, "Are they the result of brainwashing?" Martyrs bother me. I think they're often brainwashed. Muslim martyrs, Hindu martyrs, Buddhist martyrs, Christian martyrs, they are brainwashed!

They've got an idea in their heads that they must die, that death is a great thing. They feel nothing, they go right in. But not all of them, so listen to me properly. I didn't say *all* of them, but I wouldn't exclude the possibility. Lots of communists get brainwashed (you're ready to believe that). They're so brainwashed they're ready to die. I sometimes say to myself that the process that we use for making, for example, a St. Francis Xavier could be exactly the same process used for producing terrorists. You can have a man go on a thirty-day retreat and come out all aflame with the love of Christ, yet without the slightest bit of self-awareness. None. He could be a big pain. He thinks he's a great saint. I don't mean to slander Francis Xavier, who probably was a great saint, but he was a difficult man to live with. You know he was a lousy superior, he really was! Do a historical investigation. Ignatius always had to step in to undo the harm that this good man was doing by his intolerance. You need to be pretty intolerant to achieve what he achieved. Go, go, go, go—no matter how many corpses fall by the wayside. Some critics of Francis Xavier claim exactly that. He used to dismiss men from our Society and they'd appeal to Ignatius, who would say, "Come to Rome and we'll talk about it." And Ignatius surreptitiously got them in again. How much self-awareness was there in this situation? Who are we to judge, we don't know.

I'm not saying there's no such thing as pure motivation. I'm saying that ordinarily everything we do is in our self-interest. Everything. When you do something for the love of Christ, is that selfishness? Yes. When you're doing something for the love of anybody, it is in your self-interest. I'll have to explain that.

Suppose you happen to live in Phoenix and you feed over five hundred children a day. That gives you a good feeling? Well, would you expect it to give you a bad feeling? But sometimes it does. And that is because there are some people who do things so that they won't *have to have a bad feeling*. And they call *that* charity. They act out of guilt. That isn't love. But, thank God, you do things for people and it's pleasurable. Wonderful! You're a healthy individual because you're *self-interested*. That's healthy.

Let me summarize what I was saying about selfless charity. I said there were two types of selfishness; maybe I should have said three. First, when I do something, or rather, when I give myself the pleasure of pleasing myself; second, when I give myself the pleasure of pleasing others. Don't take pride in that. Don't think you're a great person. You're a very ordinary person, but you've got refined tastes. Your taste is good, not the quality of your spirituality. When you were a child, you liked Coca-Cola; now you've grown older and you appreciate chilled beer on a hot day. You've got better tastes now. When you were a child, you loved chocolates; now you're older, you enjoy a symphony, you enjoy a poem. You've got better tastes. But you're getting your pleasure all the same, except now it's in the pleasure of pleasing others. Then you've got the third type, which is the worst: when you do something good so that you won't get a bad feeling. It doesn't give you a good feeling to do it; it gives you a bad feeling to do it. You hate it. You're making loving sacrifices but you're grumbling. Ha! How little you know of yourself if you think you don't do things this way.

If I had a dollar for every time I did things that gave me

a bad feeling, I'd be a millionaire by now. You know how it goes. "Could I meet you tonight, Father?" "Yes, come on in!" I don't want to meet him and I hate meeting him. I want to watch that TV show tonight, but how do I say no to him? I don't have the guts to say no. "Come on in," and I'm thinking, "Oh God, I've got to put up with this pain."

It doesn't give me a good feeling to meet with him and it doesn't give me a good feeling to say no to him, so I choose the lesser of the two evils and I say, "O.K., come on in." I'm going to be happy when this thing is over and I'll be able to take my smile off, but I start the session with him: "How are you?" "Wonderful," he says, and he goes on and on about how he loves that workshop, and I'm thinking, "Oh God, when is he going to come to the point?" Finally he comes to the point, and I metaphorically slam him against the wall and say, "Well, any fool could solve that kind of problem," and I send him out. "Whew! Got rid of him," I say. And the next morning at breakfast (because I'm feeling I was so rude) I go up to him and say, "How's life?" And he answers, "Pretty good." And he adds, "You know, what you said to me last night was a real help. Can I meet you today, after lunch?" Oh God!

That's the worst kind of charity, when you're doing something so you won't get a bad feeling. You don't have the guts to say you want to be left alone. You want people to think you're a good priest! When you say, "I don't like hurting people," I say, "Come off it! I don't believe you." I don't believe anyone who says that he or she does not like hurting people. We love to hurt people, especially some people. We love it. And when someone else is doing the hurting we rejoice in it. But we don't want to do the hurting ourselves because *we'll* get hurt! Ah, there it is. If we do the hurting, others will have a bad opinion of us. They won't like us, they'll talk against us and we don't like that!

WHAT'S <u>ON YOUR</u> MIND?

Life is a banquet. And the tragedy is that most people are starving to death. That's what I'm really talking about. There's a nice story about some people who were on a raft off the coast of Brazil perishing from thirst. They had no idea that the water they were floating on was fresh water. The river was coming out into the sea with such force that it went out for a couple of miles, so they had fresh water right there where they were. But they had no idea. In the same way, we're surrounded with joy, with happiness, with love. Most people have no idea of this whatsoever. The reason: They're brainwashed. The reason: They're hypnotized; they're asleep. Imagine a stage magician who hypnotizes someone so that the person sees what is not there and does not see what is there. That's what it's all about. Repent and accept the good news. Repent! Wake up! Don't weep for your sins. Why weep for sins that you committed when you were asleep? Are you going to cry because of what you did in your hypnotized state? Why do you want to identify with a person like this? Wake up! Wake up! Repent! Put on a new mind. Take on a new way of looking at things! For "the kingdom is here!" It's the rare Christian who takes that seriously. I said to you that the first thing you need to do is wake up, to face the fact that you don't like being woken up. You'd much rather have all of the things which you were hypnotized into believing are so precious to you, so important to you, so important for your life and your survival. Second, understand. Understand that maybe you've got the wrong ideas and it is these ideas that are influencing your life and making it the mess that it is and keeping you asleep. Ideas about love, ideas about freedom, ideas about happiness, and so forth. And it isn't easy to listen to someone who would challenge those ideas of yours which have come to be so precious to you.

There have been some interesting studies in brainwashing. It has been shown that you're brainwashed when you take on or "introject" an idea that isn't yours, that is someone else's. And the funny thing is that you'll be ready to die for this idea. Isn't that strange? The first test of whether you've been brainwashed and have introjected convictions and beliefs occurs the moment they're attacked. You feel stunned, you react emotionally. That's a pretty good sign—not infallible, but a pretty good sign—that we're dealing with brainwashing. You're ready to die for an idea that never was yours. Terrorists or saints (so called) take on an idea, swallow it whole, and are ready to die for it. It's not easy to listen, especially when you get emotional about an idea. And even when you don't get emotional about it, it's not easy to listen; you're always listening from your programming, from your conditioning, from your hypnotic state. You frequently interpret everything that's being said in terms of your hypnotic state or your conditioning or your programming. Like this girl who's listening to a lecture on agriculture and says, "Excuse me, sir, you know I agree with you completely that the best manure is aged horse manure. Would you tell us how old the horse should optimally be?" See where she's coming from? We all have our positions, don't we? And we listen *from* those positions. "Henry, how you've changed! You were so tall and you've grown so short. You were so well built and you've grown so thin. You were so fair and you've become so dark. What happened to you, Henry?" Henry says, "I'm not Henry. I'm John." "Oh, you changed your name too!" How do you get people like that to listen?

The most difficult thing in the world is to listen, to see. We don't want to see. Do you think a capitalist wants to see what is good in the communist system? Do you think a communist wants to see what is good and healthy in the capitalist system? Do you think a rich man wants to look at poor people? We don't want to look, because if we do, we may change. We don't want to look. If you look, you lose control of the life that you are so precariously holding together. And so in order to wake up, the one thing you need the most is not energy, or strength, or youthfulness, or even great intelligence. The one thing you need most of all is the readiness to learn something new. The chances that you will wake up are in direct proportion to the amount of truth you can take without running away. How much are you ready to take? How much of everything you've held dear are you ready to have shattered, without running away? How ready are you to think of something unfamiliar?

The first reaction is one of fear. It's not that we fear the unknown. You cannot fear something that you do not know. Nobody is afraid of the unknown. What you really fear is the loss of the known. That's what you fear.

By way of an example, I made the point that everything we do is tainted with selfishness. That isn't easy to hear. But think now for a minute, let's go a little deeper into that. If everything you do comes from self-interest—enlightened or otherwise—how does that make you feel about all your charity and all your good deeds? What happens to those? Here's a little exercise for you. Think of all the good deeds you've done, or of some of them (because I'm only giving you a few seconds). Now understand that they really sprang from self-interest, whether you knew it or not. What happens to your pride? What happens to your vanity? What happens to that good feeling you gave yourself, that pat on the back every time you did something that you thought was so charitable? It gets flattened out, doesn't it? What happens to that looking down your nose at your neighbor who you thought was so selfish? The whole thing changes, doesn't it? "Well," you say, "my neighbor has coarser tastes than I do." You're the more dangerous person, you really are. Jesus Christ seems to have had less trouble with the other type than with your type. Much less trouble. He ran into trouble with people who were really convinced they were good. Other types didn't seem to give him much trouble at all, the ones who were openly selfish and knew it. Can you see how liberating that is? Hey, wake up! It's liberating. It's wonderful! Are you feeling depressed? Maybe you are. Isn't it wonderful to realize you're no better than anybody else in this world? Isn't it wonderful? Are you disappointed? Look what we've brought to light! What happens to your vanity? You'd like to give yourself a good feeling that you're better than others. But look how we brought a fallacy to light!

GOOD, BAD, OR LUCKY

To me, selfishness seems to come out of an instinct for self-preservation, which is our deepest and first instinct. How can we opt for selflessness? It would be almost like opting for nonbeing. To me, it would seem to be the same thing as nonbeing. Whatever it is, I'm saying: Stop feeling bad about being selfish; we're all the same. Someone once had a terribly beautiful thing to say about Jesus. This person wasn't even Christian. He said, "The lovely thing about Jesus was that he was so at home with sinners, because he understood that he wasn't one bit better than they were." We differ from others—from criminals, for example—only in what we do or don't do, *not in what we are*. The only difference between Jesus and those others was that he was awake and they weren't. Look at people who win the lottery. Do they say, "I'm so proud to accept this prize, not for myself, but for my nation and my society." Does anybody talk like that when they win the lottery? No. Because they were *lucky, lucky*. So they won the lottery, first prize. Anything to be proud of in that?

In the same way, if you achieved enlightenment, you would do so in the interest of self and you would be lucky. Do you want to glory in that? What's there to glory about? Can't you see how utterly stupid it is to be vain about your good deeds? The Pharisee wasn't an evil man, he was a stupid man. He was stupid, not evil. He didn't stop to think. Someone once said, "I dare not stop to think, because if I did, I wouldn't know how to get started again."

OUR ILLUSION ABOUT OTHERS

So if you stop to think, you would see that there's nothing to be very proud of after all. What does this do to your relationship with people? What are you complaining about? A young man came to complain that his girlfriend had let him down, that she had played false. What are you complaining about? Did you expect any better? Expect the worst, you're dealing with selfish people. You're the idiot— you glorified her, didn't you? You thought she was a princess, you thought people were nice. They're not! They're

PROJECTING

not nice. They're as bad as you are—bad, you understand? They're asleep like you. And what do you think they are going to seek? Their own self-interest, exactly like you. No difference. Can you imagine how liberating it is that you'll never be disillusioned again, never be disappointed again? You'll never feel let down again. Never feel rejected. Want to wake up? You want happiness? You want freedom? Here it is: Drop your false ideas. See through people. If you see through yourself, you will see through everyone. Then you will love them. Otherwise you spend the whole time grappling with your wrong notions of them, with your illusions that are constantly crashing against reality.

It's probably too startling for many of you to understand that everyone except the very rare awakened person can be *expected* to be selfish and to seek his or her own self-interest whether in coarse or in refined ways. This leads you to see that there's nothing to be disappointed about, nothing to be disillusioned about. If you had been in touch with reality all along, you would never have been disappointed. But you chose to paint people in glowing colors; you chose not to see through human beings because you chose not to see through yourself. So you're paying the price now.

Before we discuss this, let me tell you a story. Somebody once asked, "What is enlightenment like? What is awakening like?" It's like the tramp in London who was settling in for the night. He'd hardly been able to get a crust of bread to eat. Then he reaches this embankment on the river Thames. There was a slight drizzle, so he huddled in his old tattered cloak. He was about to go to sleep when suddenly a chauffeur-driven Rolls-Royce pulls up. Out of the car steps a beautiful young lady who says to him, "My poor man, are you planning on spending the night here on this embankment?" And the tramp says, "Yes." She says, "I won't have it. You're coming to my house and you're going to spend a comfortable night and you're going to get a good dinner." She insists on his getting into the car. Well, they ride out of London and get to a place where she has a sprawling mansion with large grounds. They are ushered in by the butler, to whom she says, "James, please make sure he's put in the servants' quarters and treated well." Which is what James does. The young lady had undressed and was about to go to bed when she suddenly remembers her guest for the night. So she slips something on and pads along the corridor to the servants' quarters. She sees a little chink of light from the room where the tramp was put up. She taps lightly at the door, opens it, and finds the man awake. She says, "What's the trouble, my good man, didn't you get a good meal?" He said, "Never had a better meal in my life, lady." "Are you warm enough?" He says, "Yes, lovely warm bed." Then she says, "Maybe you need a little company. Why don't you move over a bit." And she comes closer to him and he moves over and falls right into the Thames.

Ha! You didn't expect that one! Enlightenment! Enlightenment! Wake up. When you're ready to exchange your illusions for reality, when you're ready to exchange your dreams for facts, that's the way you find it all. That's where life finally becomes meaningful. Life becomes beautiful.

There's a story about Ramirez. He is old and living up

there in his castle on a hill. He looks out the window (he's in bed and paralyzed) and he sees his enemy. Old as he is, leaning on a cane, his enemy is climbing up the hill—slowly, painfully. It takes him about two and a half hours to get up the hill. There's nothing Ramirez can do because the servants have the day off. So his enemy opens the door, comes straight to the bedroom, puts his hand inside his cloak, and pulls out a gun. He says, "At last, Ramirez, we're going to settle scores!" Ramirez tries his level best to talk him out of it. He says, "Come on, Borgia, you can't do that. You know I'm no longer the man who ill-treated you as that youngster years ago, and you're no longer that youngster. Come off it!" "Oh no," says his enemy, "your sweet words aren't going to deter me from this divine mission of mine. It's revenge I want and there's nothing you can do about it." And Ramirez says, "But there is!" "What?" asks his enemy. "I can wake up," says Ramirez. And he did; he woke up! That's what enlightenment is like. When someone tells you, "There is nothing you can do about it," you say, "There is, I can wake up!" All of a sudden, life is no longer the nightmare that it has seemed. Wake up!

Somebody came up to me with a question. What do you think the question was? He asked me, "Are you enlightened?" What do you think my answer was? What does it matter!

You want a better answer? My answer would be: "How would I know? How would you know? What does it matter?" You know something? If you want anything too badly, you're in big trouble. You know something else? If I were enlightened and you listened to me because I was enlightened, then you're in big trouble. Are you ready to be brainwashed by someone who's enlightened? You can be brainwashed by anybody, you know. What does it matter whether someone's enlightened or not? But see, we want to lean on someone, don't we? We want to lean on anybody we think has arrived. We love to hear that people have arrived. It gives us hope, doesn't it? What do you want to hope for? Isn't that another form of desire?

You want to hope for something better than what you have right now, don't you? Otherwise you wouldn't be hoping. But then, you forget that you have it all right now anyway, and you don't know it. Why not concentrate on the now instead of hoping for better times in the future? Why not understand the now instead of forgetting it and hoping for the future? Isn't the future just another trap?

SELF-OBSERVATION

The only way someone can be of help to you is in challenging your ideas. If you're ready to listen and if you're ready to be challenged, there's one thing that you can do, but *no one can help you.* What is this most important thing of all? It's called self-observation. No one can help you there. No one can give you a method. No one can show you a technique. The moment you pick up a technique, you're programmed again. But self-observation—watching yourself—is important. It is not the same as self-absorption. Self-absorption is self-preoccupation, where you're concerned about yourself, worried about yourself. I'm talking about self-*observation*. What's that? It means to watch everything in you and around you as far as possible and watch it as if it were happening to someone else. What does that last sentence mean? It means that you do not personalize what is happening to you. It means that you look at things as if you have no connection with them whatsoever.

The reason you suffer from your depression and your anxieties is that you identify with them. You say, "I'm depressed." But that is false. You are not depressed. If you want to be accurate, you might say, "I am experiencing a depression right now." But you can hardly say, "I am depressed." You are not your depression. That is but a strange kind of trick of the mind, a strange kind of illusion. You have deluded yourself into thinking—though you are not aware of it—that you *are* your depression, that you *are* your anxiety, that you *are* your joy or the thrills that you have. "I am delighted!" You certainly are not delighted. Delight may be *in* you right now, but wait around, it will change; it won't last: it never lasts; it keeps changing: it's always changing. Clouds come and go: some of them are black and some white, some of them are large, others small. If we want to follow the analogy, you would be the sky, observing the clouds. You are a passive, detached observer. That's shocking, particularly to someone in the Western culture.

You're not interfering. Don't interfere. Don't "fix" anything. Watch! Observe!

The trouble with people is that they're busy fixing things they don't even understand. We're always fixing things, aren't we? It never strikes us that things don't need to be fixed. They really don't. This is a great illumination. They need to be understood. If you understood them, they'd change.

❧
AWARENESS WITHOUT EVALUATING EVERYTHING

Do you want to change the world? How about beginning with yourself? How about being transformed yourself first? But how do you achieve that? Through observation. Through understanding. With no interference or judgment on your part. Because what you judge you cannot understand.

When you say of someone, "He's a communist," understanding has stopped at that moment. You slapped a label on him. "She's a capitalist." Understanding has stopped at that moment. You slapped a label on her, and if the label carries undertones of approval or disapproval, so much the worse! How are you going to understand what you disapprove of, or what you approve of, for that matter? All of this sounds like a new world, doesn't it? No judgment, no commentary, no attitude: one simply observes, one studies, one watches,

without the desire to change what is. Because if you desire
to change what is into what you think *should* be, you no
longer understand. A dog trainer attempts to understand a
dog so that he can train the dog to perform certain tricks. A
scientist observes the behavior of ants with no further end in
view than to study ants, to learn as much as possible about
them. He has no other aim. He's not attempting to train
them or get anything out of them. He's interested in ants, he
wants to learn as much as possible about them. That's his
attitude. The day you attain a posture like that, you will
experience a miracle. You will change—effortlessly, cor-
rectly. Change will happen, you will not have to bring it
about. As the life of awareness settles on your darkness,
whatever is evil will disappear. Whatever is good will be
fostered. You will have to experience that for yourself.

But this calls for a disciplined mind. And when I say
disciplined, I'm not talking about effort. I'm talking about
something else. Have you ever studied an athlete. His or her
whole life is sports, but what a disciplined life he or she
leads. And look at a river as it moves toward the sea. It
creates its own banks that contain it. When there's something within you that moves in the right direction, it creates
its own discipline. The moment you get bitten by the bug
of awareness. Oh, it's so delightful! It's the most delightful
thing in the world; the most important, the most delightful.
There's nothing so important in the world as awakening.
Nothing! And, of course, it is also discipline in its own
way.

There's nothing so delightful as being aware. Would you

rather live in darkness? Would you rather act and not be aware of your actions, talk and not be aware of your words? Would you rather listen to people and not be aware of what you're hearing, or see things and not be aware of what you're looking at? The great Socrates said, "The unaware life is not worth living." That's a self-evident truth. Most people don't live aware lives. They live mechanical lives, mechanical thoughts—generally somebody else's—mechanical emotions, mechanical actions, mechanical reactions. Do you want to see how mechanical you really are? "My, that's a lovely shirt you're wearing." You feel good hearing that. For a shirt, for heaven's sake! You feel proud of yourself when you hear that. People come over to my center in India and they say, "What a lovely place, these lovely trees" (for which I'm not responsible at all), "this lovely climate." And already I'm feeling good, until I catch myself feeling good, and I say, "Hey, can you imagine anything as stupid as that?" I'm not responsible for those trees; I wasn't responsible for choosing the location. I didn't order the weather; it just happened. But "me" got in there, so I'm feeling good. I'm feeling good about "my" culture and "my" nation. How stupid can you get? I mean that. I'm told my great Indian culture has produced all these mystics. I didn't produce them. I'm not responsible for them. Or they tell me, "That country of yours and its poverty—it's disgusting." I feel ashamed. But I didn't create it. What's going on? Did you ever stop to think? People tell you, "I think you're very charming," so I feel wonderful. I get a positive stroke (that's why they call it I'm O.K., you're

O.K.). I'm going to write a book someday and the title will be *I'm an Ass, You're an Ass*. That's the most liberating, wonderful thing in the world, when you openly admit you're an ass. It's wonderful. When people tell me, "You're wrong." I say, "What can you expect of an ass?"

Disarmed, everybody has to be disarmed. In the final liberation, I'm an ass, you're an ass. Normally the way it goes, I press a button and you're up; I press another button and you're down. And you like that. How many people do you know who are unaffected by praise or blame? That isn't human, we say. Human means that you have to be a little monkey, so everybody can twist your tail, and you do whatever you *ought* to be doing. But is that human? If you find me charming, it means that right now you're in a good mood, nothing more.

It also means that I fit your shopping list. We all carry a shopping list around, and it's as though you've got to measure up to this list—tall, um, dark, um, handsome, according to *my* tastes. "I like the sound of his voice." You say, "I'm in love." You're not in love, you silly ass. Any time you're in love—I hesitate to say this—you're being particularly asinine. Sit down and watch what's happening to you. You're running away from yourself. You want to escape. Somebody once said, "Thank God for reality, *and* for the means to escape from it." So that's what's going on. We are so mechanical, so controlled. We write books about being controlled and how wonderful it is to be controlled and how necessary it is that people tell you you're O.K. Then you'll have a good feeling about yourself. How wonderful it is to be in prison! Or as somebody said to me yesterday, to be in your cage. Do you like being in prison? Do you like being controlled? Let me tell you something: If you ever let yourself feel good when people tell you that you're O.K., you are preparing yourself to feel bad when they tell you you're not good. As long as you live to fulfill other people's expectations, you better watch what you wear, how you comb your hair, whether your shoes are polished —in short, whether you live up to every damned expectation of theirs. Do you call that human?

This is what you'll discover when you observe yourself! You'll be horrified! The fact of the matter is that you're neither O.K. nor not O.K. You may fit the current mood or trend or fashion! Does that mean you've become O.K.? Does your O.K.-ness depend on that? Does it depend on what people think of you? Jesus Christ must have been pretty "not O.K." by those standards. You're not O.K. and you're not not O.K., you're you. I hope that is going to be the big discovery, at least for some of you. If three or four of you make this discovery during these days we spend together, my, what a wonderful thing! Extraordinary! Cut out all the O.K. stuff and the not-O.K. stuff; cut out all the judgments and simply observe, watch. You'll make great discoveries. These discoveries will change you. You won't have to make the slightest effort, believe me.

This reminds me of this fellow in London after the war. He's sitting with a parcel wrapped in brown paper in his lap; it's a big, heavy object. The bus conductor comes up to him and says, "What do you have on your lap there?" And the man says, "This is an unexploded bomb. We dug it out of the garden and I'm taking it to the police station." The conductor says, "You don't want to carry that on your lap. Put it under the seat."

Psychology and spirituality (as we generally understand it) transfer the bomb from your lap to under your seat. They don't really solve your problems. They exchange your problems for other problems. Has that ever struck you? You had a problem, now you exchange it for another one. It's always going to be that way until we solve the problem called "you."

🍎
THE ILLUSION OF REWARDS

Until then, we're going to get nowhere. The great mystics and masters in the East will say, "Who are *you?*" Many think the most important question in the world is: "Who is Jesus Christ?" Wrong!

Many think it is: "Does God exist?" Wrong! Many think it is: "Is there a life after death?" Wrong! Nobody seems to be grappling with the problem of: Is there a life *before* death? Yet my experience is that it's precisely the ones who don't know what to do with *this* life who are all hot and bothered about what they are going to do with *another* life. One sign that you're awakened is that you don't give a damn about what's going to happen in the next life. You're not bothered about it; you don't care. You are not interested, period.

Do you know what eternal life is? You think it's everlasting life. But your own theologians will tell you that that is crazy, because everlasting is still within time. It is time perduring forever. Eternal means timeless—no time. The human mind cannot understand that. The human mind can understand time and can deny time. What is timeless is beyond our comprehension. Yet the mystics tell us that eternity is right now. How's that for good news? It is right now. People are so distressed when I tell them to forget their past. They are so proud of their past. Or they are so ashamed of their past. They're crazy! Just drop it! When you hear "Repent for your past," realize it's a great religious distraction from waking up. Wake up! That's what repent means. Not "weep for your sins." Wake up! Understand, stop all the crying. Understand! Wake up!

❦
FINDING YOURSELF

The great masters tell us that the most important question in the world is: "Who am I?" Or rather: "What is 'I'?" What is this thing I call "I"? What is this thing I call self? You mean you understood everything else in the world and you didn't understand this? You mean you understood astronomy and black holes and quasars and you picked up computer science, and you don't know who you are? My, you are still asleep. You are a sleeping scientist. You mean you understood what Jesus Christ is and you don't know who you are? How do you know that you have understood Jesus Christ? Who is the person doing the understanding? Find that out first. That's the foundation of everything, isn't it? It's because we haven't understood this that we've got all these stupid religious people involved in all these stupid religious wars—Muslims fighting against Jews, Protestants fighting Catholics, and all the rest of that rubbish. They don't know who they are, because if they did, there wouldn't be wars. Like the little girl who says to a little boy, "Are you a Presbyterian?" And he says, "No, we belong to another abomination!"

But what I'd like to stress right now is self-observation. You are listening to me, but are you picking up any other sounds besides the sound of my voice as you listen to me? Are you aware of *your* reactions as you listen to me? If you aren't, you're going to be brainwashed. Or else you are going to be influenced by forces within you of which you have no awareness at all. And even if you're aware of how you react to me, are you simultaneously aware of where your reaction is coming from? Maybe you are not listening to me at all; maybe your daddy is listening to me. Do you think that's possible? Of course it is. Again and again in my therapy groups I come across people who aren't there at all. Their daddy is there, their mommy is there, but they're not there. They never were there. "I live now, not I, but my daddy lives in me." Well, that's absolutely, literally true. I could take you apart piece by piece and ask, "Now, this sentence, does it come from Daddy, Mommy, Grandma, Grandpa, whom?"

Who's living in you? It's pretty horrifying when you come to know that. You think you are free, but there probably isn't a gesture, a thought, an emotion, an attitude, a belief in you that isn't coming from someone else. Isn't that horrible? And you don't know it. Talk about a mechanical life that was stamped into you. You feel pretty strongly about certain things, and you think it is you who are feeling strongly about them, but are you really? It's going to take a lot of awareness for you to understand that perhaps this thing you call "I" is simply a conglomeration of your past experiences, of your conditioning and programming.

That's painful. In fact, when you're beginning to awaken, you experience a great deal of pain. It's painful to see your illusions being shattered. Everything that you thought you had built up crumbles and that's painful. That's what repentance is all about; that's what waking up is all about. So how about taking a minute, right where you're sitting now, to be aware, even as I talk, of what you're feeling in your body, and what's going on in your mind, and what your emotional state is like? How about being aware of the blackboard, if your eyes are open, and the color of these walls and the material they're made of? How about being aware of my face and the reaction you have to this face of mine? Because you have a reaction whether you're aware of it or not. And it probably isn't your reaction, but one you were conditioned to have. And how about being aware of some of the things I just said, although that wouldn't be awareness, because that's just memory now.

Be aware of your presence in this room. Say to yourself, "I'm in this room." It's as if you were outside yourself looking at yourself. Notice a slightly different feeling than if you were looking at things in the room. Later we'll ask, "Who is this person who is doing the looking?" I am looking at me. What's an "I"? What's "me"? For the time being it's enough that I watch me, but if you find yourself condemning yourself or approving yourself, don't stop the condemnation and don't stop the judgment or approval, just watch it. I'm condemning me; I'm disapproving of me; I'm approving of me. Just look at it, period. Don't try to change it! Don't say, "Oh, we were told not to do this." Just observe what's going on. As I said to you before, self-observation means watching—observing whatever is going on in you and around you as if it were happening to someone else.

STRIPPING DOWN TO THE "I"

I suggest another exercise now. Would you write down on a piece of paper any brief way you would describe yourself —for example, businessman, priest, human being, Catholic, Jew, anything.

Some write, I notice, things like, fruitful, searching pilgrim, competent, alive, impatient, centered, flexible, reconciler, lover, member of the human race, overly structured. This is the fruit, I trust, of observing yourself. As if you were watching another person.

But notice, you've got "I" observing "me." This is an interesting phenomenon that has never ceased to cause wonder to philosophers, mystics, scientists, psychologists, that the "I" can observe "me." It would seem that animals are not able to do this at all. It would seem that one needs a certain amount of intelligence to be able to do this. What I'm going to give you now is not metaphysics; it is not philosophy. It is plain observation and common sense. The great mystics of the East are really referring to that "I," not to the "me." As a matter of fact, some of these mystics tell us that we begin first with things, with an awareness of things; then we move on to an awareness of thoughts (that's the "me"); and finally we get to awareness of the thinker. Things, thoughts, thinker. What we're really searching for is the thinker. Can the thinker know himself? Can I know what "I" is? Some of these mystics reply, "Can the knife cut itself? Can the tooth bite itself? Can the eye see itself? Can the 'I' know itself?" But I am concerned with something infinitely more practical right now, and that is with deciding what the "I" is *not*. I'll go as slowly as possible because the consequences are devastating. Terrific or terrifying, depending on your point of view.

Listen to this: Am I my thoughts, the thoughts that I am thinking? No. Thoughts come and go; I am not my thoughts. Am I my body? They tell us that millions of cells in our body are changed or are renewed every minute, so that by the end of seven years we don't have a single living cell in our body that was there seven years before. Cells come and go. Cells arise and die. But "I" seems to persist. So am I my body? Evidently not!

"I" is something other and more than the body. You might say the body is part of "I," but it is a changing part. It keeps moving, it keeps changing. We have the same name for it but it constantly changes. Just as we have the same name for Niagara Falls, but Niagara Falls is constituted by water that is constantly changing. We use the same name for an ever-changing reality.

How about my name? Is "I" my name? Evidently not, because I can change my name without changing the "I." How about my career? How about my beliefs? I say I am a Catholic, a Jew—is that an essential part of "I"? When I move from one religion to another, has the "I" changed? Do I have a new "I" or is it the same "I" that has changed? In other words, is my name an essential part of me, of the "I"? Is my religion an essential part of the "I"? I mentioned the little girl who says to the boy, "Are you a Presbyterian?" Well, somebody told me another story, about Paddy. Paddy was walking down the street in Belfast and he discovers a gun pressing against the back of his head and a voice says, "Are you Catholic or Protestant?" Well, Paddy has to do some pretty fast thinking. He says, "I'm a Jew." And he hears a voice say, "I've got to be the luckiest Arab in the whole of Belfast." Labels are so important to us. "I am a Republican," we say. But are you really? You can't mean that when you switch parties you have a new "I." Isn't it the same old "I" with new political convictions? I remember hearing about a man who asks his friend, "Are you planning to vote Republican?" The friend says, "No, I'm planning to vote Democratic. My father was a Democrat, my grandfather was a Democrat, and my great-grandfather was a Democrat." The man says, "That is crazy logic. I mean, if your father was a horse thief, and your grandfather was a horse thief, and your great-grandfather was a horse thief, what would you be?" "Ah," the friend answered, "then I'd be a Republican."

We spend so much of our lives reacting to labels, our own and others'. We identify the labels with the "I." Catholic and Protestant are frequent labels. There was a man who went to the priest and said, "Father, I want you to say a Mass for my dog." The priest was indignant. "What do you mean, say a Mass for your dog?" "It's my pet dog," said the man. "I loved that dog and I'd like you to offer a Mass for him." The priest said, "We don't offer Masses for dogs here. You might try the denomination down the street. Ask them if they might have a service for you." As the man was leaving, he said to the priest, "Too bad. I really loved that dog. I was planning to offer a million-dollar stipend for the Mass." And the priest said, "Wait a minute, you never told me your dog was Catholic."

When you're caught up in labels, what value do these labels have, as far as the "I" is concerned? Could we say that "I" is none of the labels we attach to it? Labels belong to "me." What constantly changes is "me." Does "I" ever change? Does the observer ever change? The fact is that no matter what labels you think of (except perhaps human being) you should apply them to "me." "I" is none of these things. So when you step out of yourself and observe "me," you no longer identify with "me." Suffering exists in "me," so when you identify "I" with "me," suffering begins.

Say that you are afraid or desirous or anxious. When "I" does not *identify* with money, or name, or nationality, or persons, or friends, or any quality, the "I" is never threatened. It can be very active, but it isn't threatened. Think of anything that caused or is causing you pain or worry or anxiety. First, can you pick up the desire under that suffering, that there's something you desire very keenly or else you wouldn't be suffering. What is that desire? Second, it isn't simply a desire; there's an *identification* there. You have somehow said to yourself, "The well-being of 'I,' almost the existence of 'I,' is tied up with this desire." All suffering is caused by my identifying myself with something, whether that something is within me or outside of me.

❦

NEGATIVE FEELINGS TOWARD OTHERS

At one of my conferences, someone made the following observation:

"I want to share with you something wonderful that happened to me. I went to the movies and I was working shortly after that and I was really having trouble with three people in my life. So I said, 'All right, just like I learned at the movies, I'm going to come outside myself.' For a couple of hours, I got in touch with my feelings, with how badly I felt toward these three people. I said, 'I really hate those people.' Then I said, 'Jesus, what can you do about all that?' A little while later I began to cry, because I realized that Jesus died for those very people and they couldn't help how they were, anyway. That afternoon I had to go to the office, where I spoke to those people. I told them what my problem was and they agreed with me. I wasn't mad at them and I didn't hate them anymore."

Anytime you have a negative feeling toward anyone, you're living in an illusion. There's something seriously wrong with you. You're not seeing reality. Something inside of you has to change. But what do we generally do when we have a negative feeling? "He is to blame, she is to blame. She's got to change." No! The world's all right. The one who has to change is *you*.

One of you told of working in an institution. During a staff meeting someone would inevitably say, "The food stinks around here," and the regular dietitian would go into orbit. She has identified with the food. She is saying, "Anyone who attacks the food attacks me; I feel threatened." But the "I" is never threatened; it's only the "me" that is threatened.

But suppose you witness some out-and-out injustice, something that is obviously and objectively wrong. Would it not be a proper reaction to say this should not be happening? Should you somehow want to involve yourself in correcting a situation that's wrong? Someone's injuring a child and you see abuse going on. How about that kind of thing? I hope you did not assume that I was saying you shouldn't do anything. I said that if you didn't have negative feelings you'd be much more effective, *much* more effective. Because when negative feelings come in, you go blind. "Me" steps into the picture, and everything gets fouled up. Where we had one problem on our hands before, now we have two problems. Many wrongly assume that not having negative feelings like anger and resentment and hate means that you do nothing about a situation. Oh no, oh no! You are not affected emotionally but you spring into action. You become very sensitive to things and people around you. What kills the sensitivity is what many people would call the conditioned self: when you so identify with "me" that there's too much of "me" in it for you to see things objectively, with detachment. It's very important that when you swing into action, you be able to see things with detachment. But negative emotions prevent that.

What, then, would we call the kind of passion that motivates or activates energy into doing something about objective evils? Whatever it is, it is not a *reaction;* it is action.

Some of you wonder if there is a gray area before something becomes an attachment, before identification sets in. Say a friend dies. It seems right and very human to feel some sadness about that. But what reaction? Self-pity? What would you be grieving about? Think about that. What I'm saying is going to sound terrible to you, but I told you, I'm coming from another world. Your reaction is *personal* loss, right? Feeling sorry for "me" or for other people your friend might have brought joy to. But that means you're feeling sorry for other people who are feeling sorry for themselves. If they're not feeling sorry for themselves, what would they be feeling sorry for? We never feel grief when we lose something that we have allowed to be free, that we have never attempted to possess. Grief is a sign that I made my happiness depend on this thing or person, at least to some extent. We're so accustomed to hear the opposite of this that what I say sounds inhuman, doesn't it?

❦

ON <u>DEPENDENCE</u>

But it's what all the mystics in the past have been telling us. I'm not saying that "me," the conditioned-self, will not sometimes fall into its usual patterns. That's the way we've been conditioned. But it raises the question whether it is conceivable to live a life in which you would be so totally alone that you would depend on no one.

We all depend on one another for all kinds of things, don't we? We depend on the butcher, the baker, the candlestick maker. Interdependence. That's fine! We set up society this way and we allot different functions to different people for the welfare of everyone, so that we will function better and live more effectively—at least we hope so. But to depend on another psychologically—to depend on another emotionally—what does that imply? It means to depend on another human being for my happiness.

Think about that. Because if you do, the next thing you will be doing, whether you're aware of it or not, is *demanding* that other people contribute to your happiness. Then there will be a next step—fear, fear of loss, fear of alienation, fear of rejection, mutual control. Perfect love casts out fear. Where there is love there are no demands, no expectations, no dependency. I do not demand that you make me happy; my happiness does not lie in you. If you were to leave me, I will not feel sorry for myself; I enjoy your company immensely, but I do not cling.

I enjoy it on a nonclinging basis. What I really enjoy is not you; it's something that's greater than both you and me. It is something that I discovered, a kind of symphony, a kind of orchestra that plays one melody in your presence, but when you depart, the orchestra doesn't stop. When I meet someone else, it plays another melody, which is also very delightful. And when I'm alone, it continues to play. There's a great repertoire and it never ceases to play.

That's what awakening is all about. That's also why we're hypnotized, brainwashed, asleep. It seems terrifying to ask, but can you be said to love me if you cling to me and will not let me go? If you will not let me be? Can you be said to love me if you need me psychologically or emotionally for your happiness? This flies in the face of the universal teaching of all the scriptures, of all religions, of all the mystics. "How is it that we missed it for so many years?" I say to myself repeatedly. "How come I didn't see it?"

When you read those radical things in the scriptures, you begin to wonder: Is this man crazy? But after a while you begin to think everybody else is crazy. "Unless you hate your father and mother, brothers and sisters, unless you renounce and give up everything you possess, you cannot be my disciple." You must drop it all. Not physical renunciation, you understand; that's easy. When your illusions drop, you're in touch with reality at last, and believe me, you will never again be lonely, never again. Loneliness is not cured by human company. Loneliness is cured by contact with reality. Oh, I have so much to say about that. Contact with reality, dropping one's illusions, making contact with the real. Whatever it is, it has no name. We can only know it by dropping what is unreal. You can only know what aloneness is when you drop your clinging, when you drop your dependency. But the first step toward that is that you see it as desirable. If you don't see it as desirable, how will you get anywhere near it?

Think of the loneliness that is yours. Would human company ever take it away? It will only serve as a distraction. There's an emptiness inside, isn't there? And when the emptiness surfaces, what do you do? You run away, turn on the television, turn on the radio, read a book, search for human company, seek entertainment, seek distraction. Everybody does that. It's big business nowadays, an organized industry to distract us and entertain us.

HOW HAPPINESS HAPPENS

Come home to yourself. Observe yourself. That's why I said earlier that self-observation is such a delightful and extraordinary thing. After a while you don't have to make any effort, because, as illusions begin to crumble, you begin to know things that cannot be described. It's called happiness. Everything changes and you become addicted to awareness.

There's the story of the disciple who went to the master and said, "Could you give me a word of wisdom? Could you tell me something that would guide me through my days?" It was the master's day of silence, so he picked up a pad. It said, "Awareness." When the disciple saw it, he said, "This is too brief. Can you expand on it a bit?" So the master took back the pad and wrote, "Awareness, awareness, awareness." The disciple said, "Yes, but what does it mean?" The master took back the pad and wrote, "Awareness, awareness, awareness means—awareness."

That's what it is to watch yourself. No one can show you how to do it, because he would be giving you a technique, he would be programming you. But watch yourself. When you talk to someone, are you aware of it or are you simply identifying with it? When you got angry with somebody, were you aware that you were angry or were you simply identifying with your anger? Later, when you had the time, did you study your experience and attempt to understand it? Where did it come from? What brought it on? I don't know of any other way to awareness. You only change what you understand. What you do not understand and are not aware of, you repress. You don't change. But when you understand it, it changes.

I am sometimes asked, "Is this growing in awareness a gradual thing, or is it a 'whammo' kind of thing?" There are some lucky people who see this in a flash. They just become aware. There are others who keep growing into it, slowly, gradually, increasingly. They begin to see things. Illusions drop away, fantasies are peeled away, and they start to get in touch with facts. There's no general rule. There's a famous story about the lion who came upon a flock of sheep and to his amazement found a lion among the sheep. It was a lion who had been brought up by the sheep ever since he was a cub. It would bleat like a sheep and run around like a sheep. The lion went straight for him, and when the sheep-lion stood in front of the real one, he trembled in every limb. And the lion said to him, "What are you doing among these sheep?" And the sheep-lion said, "I am a sheep." And the lion said, "Oh no you're not. You're coming with me." So he took the sheep-lion to a pool and said, "Look!" And when the sheep-lion looked at his reflection in the water, he let out a mighty roar, and in that moment he was transformed. He was never the same again.

If you're lucky and the gods are gracious or if you are gifted with divine grace (use any theological expression you want), you might suddenly understand who "I" is, and you'll never be the same again, never. Nothing will ever be able to touch you again and no one will ever be able to hurt you again.

You will fear no one and you will fear nothing. Isn't that

extraordinary? You'll live like a king, like a queen. This is what it means to live like royalty. Not rubbish like getting your picture in the newspapers or having a lot of money. That's a lot of rot. You fear no one because you're perfectly content to be nobody. You don't give a damn about success or failure. They mean nothing. Honor, disgrace, they mean nothing! If you make a fool of yourself, that means nothing either. Isn't that a wonderful state to be in! Some people arrive at this goal painstakingly, step by step, through months and weeks of self-awareness. But I'll promise you this: I have not known a single person who gave time to being aware who didn't see a difference in a matter of weeks. The quality of their life changes, so they don't have to take it on faith anymore. They see it; they're different. They react differently. In fact, they react less and act more. You see things you've never seen before.

You're much more energetic, much more alive. People think that if they had no cravings, they'd be like deadwood. But in fact they'd lose their tension. Get rid of your fear of failure, your tensions about succeeding, you will be yourself. Relaxed. You wouldn't be driving with your brakes on. That's what would happen.

There's a lovely saying of Tranxu, a great Chinese sage, that I took the trouble to learn by heart. It goes: "When the archer shoots for no particular prize, he has all his skills; when he shoots to win a brass buckle, he is already nervous; when he shoots for a gold prize, he goes blind, sees two targets, and is out of his mind. His skill has not changed, but the prize divides him. He cares! He thinks more of winning than of shooting, and the need to win drains him of power." Isn't that an image of what most people are? When you're living for nothing, you've got all your skills, you've got all your energy, you're relaxed, you don't care, it doesn't matter whether you win or lose.

Now there's *human* living for you. That's what life is all about. That can only come from awareness. And in awareness you will understand that honor doesn't mean a thing. It's a social convention, that's all. That's why the mystics and the prophets didn't bother one bit about it. Honor or disgrace meant nothing to them. They were living in another world, in the world of the awakened. Success or failure meant nothing to them. They had the attitude: "I'm an ass, you're an ass, so where's the problem?"

Someone once said, "The three most difficult things for a human being are not physical feats or intellectual achievements. They are, first, returning love for hate; second, including the excluded; third, admitting that you are wrong." But these are the easiest things in the world if you haven't identified with the "me." You can say things like "I'm wrong! If you knew me better, you'd see how often I'm wrong. What would you expect from an ass?" But if I haven't identified with these aspects of "me," you can't hurt me. Initially, the old conditioning will kick in and you'll be depressed and anxious. You'll grieve, cry, and so on. "Before enlightenment, I used to be depressed: after enlightenment, I continue to be depressed." But there's a difference: I don't identify with it anymore. Do you know what a big difference that is?

You step outside of yourself and look at that depression, and don't identify with it. You don't do a thing to make it go away; you are perfectly willing to go on with your life while it passes through you and disappears. If you don't know what that means, you really have something to look forward to. And anxiety? There it comes and you're not troubled. How strange! You're anxious but you're not troubled.

Isn't that a paradox? And you're willing to let this cloud come in, because the more you fight it, the more power you give it. You're willing to observe it as it passes by. You can be happy in your anxiety. Isn't that crazy? You can be happy in your depression. But you can't have the wrong notion of happiness. Did you think happiness was excitement or thrills? That's what causes the depression. Didn't anyone tell you that? You're thrilled, all right, but you're just preparing the way for your next depression. You're thrilled but you pick up the anxiety behind that: How can I make it last? That's not happiness, that's addiction.

I wonder how many nonaddicts there are reading this book? If you're anything like the average group, there are few, very few. Don't look down your nose at the alcoholics and the drug addicts: maybe you're just as addicted as they are. The first time I got a glimpse of this new world, it was terrifying. I understood what it meant to be alone, with nowhere to rest your head, to leave everyone free and be free yourself, to be special to no one and love everyone—because love does that. It shines on good and bad alike; it makes rain fall on saints and sinners alike.

Is it possible for the rose to say, "I will give my fragrance to the good people who smell me, but I will withhold it from the bad"? Or is it possible for the lamp to say, "I will give my light to the good people in this room, but I will withhold it from the evil people"? Or can a tree say, "I'll give my shade to the good people who rest under me, but I will withhold it from the bad"? These are images of what love is about.

It's been there all along, staring us in the face in the scriptures, though we never cared to see it because we were so drowned in what our culture calls love with its love songs and poems—that isn't love at all, that's the opposite of love. That's desire and control and possessiveness. That's manipulation, and fear, and anxiety—that's not love. We were told that happiness is a smooth complexion, a holiday resort. It isn't these things, but we have subtle ways of making our happiness depend on other things, both within us and outside us. We say, "I refuse to be happy until my neurosis goes." I have good news for you: You can be happy right now, *with* the neurosis, You want even better news? There's only one reason why you're not experiencing what in India we call *anand*—bliss, bliss. There's only one reason why you're not experiencing bliss at this present moment, and it's because you're thinking or focusing on what you don't have. Otherwise you would be experiencing bliss. You're focusing on what you don't have. But, right now you have everything you need to be in bliss.

Jesus was talking horse sense to lay people, to starving

people, to poor people. He was telling them good news: It's yours for the taking, But who listens? No one's interested, they'd rather be asleep.

❧ FEAR—THE ROOT OF <u>VIOLEN</u>CE

Some say that there are only two things in the world: God and fear; love and fear are the only two things. There's only one evil in the world, fear. There's only one good in the world, love. It's sometimes called by other names. It's sometimes called happiness or freedom or peace or joy or God or whatever. But the label doesn't really matter. And there's not a single evil in the world that you cannot trace to fear. Not one.

Ignorance and fear, ignorance caused by fear, that's where all the evil comes from, that's where your violence comes from. The person who is truly nonviolent, who is incapable of violence, is the person who is fearless. It's only when you're afraid that you become angry. Think of the last time you were angry. Go ahead. Think of the last time you were angry and search for the fear behind it. What were you afraid of losing? What were you afraid would be taken from you? That's where the anger comes from. Think of an angry person, maybe someone you're afraid of. Can you see how frightened he or she is? He's really frightened, he really is. She's really frightened or she wouldn't be angry. Ultimately, there are only two things, love and fear.

In this retreat I'd rather leave it like this, unstructured and moving from one thing to another and returning to themes again and again, because that's the way to really grasp what I'm saying. If it doesn't hit you the first time, it might the second time, and what doesn't hit one person might hit another. I've got different themes, but they are all about the same thing. Call it awareness, call it love, call it spirituality or freedom or awakening or whatever. It really is the same thing.

❧

AWARENESS AND CONTACT WITH REALITY

To watch everything inside of you and outside, and when there is something happening to you, to see it as if it were happening to someone else, with no comment, no judgment, no attitude, no interference, no attempt to change, only to understand. As you do this, you'll begin to realize that increasingly you are disidentifying from "me." St. Teresa of Avila says that toward the end of her life God gave her an extraordinary grace. She doesn't use this modern expression, of course, but what it really boils down to is disidentifying from herself. If someone else has cancer and I don't know the person, I'm not all that affected. If I had love and sensitivity, maybe I'd help, but I'm not emotionally affected. If *you* have an examination to take, I'm not all that affected. I can be quite philosophical about it and say, "Well, the more you worry about it, the worse it'll get. Why not just take a good break instead of studying?" But when it's my turn to have an examination, well, that's something else, isn't it? The reason is that I've identified with "me"—with my family, my country, my possessions, my body, me. How would it be if God gave me grace not to call these things mine? I'd be detached; I'd be disidentified. That's what it means to lose the self, to deny the self, to die to self.

❦
GOOD RELIGION— THE ANTITHESIS OF UNAWARENESS

Somebody came up to me once during a conference and asked, "What about 'Our Lady of Fatima'?" What do you think of her? When I am asked questions like that, I am reminded of the story of the time they were taking the statue of Our Lady of Fatima on an airplane to a pilgrimage for worship, and as they were flying over the South of France the plane began to wobble and to shake and it looked like it was going to come apart. And the miraculous statue cried out, "Our Lady of Lourdes, pray for us!" And all was well. Wasn't it wonderful, one "Our Lady" helping another "Our Lady"?

There was also a group of a thousand people who went on a pilgrimage to Mexico City to venerate the shrine of Our Lady of Guadalupe and sat down before the statue in protest because the Bishop of the Diocese had declared "Our Lady of Lourdes" patroness of the diocese! They were sure that Our Lady of Guadalupe felt this very much, so they were doing the protest in *reparation* for the offense. That's the trouble with religion, if you don't watch out.

When I speak to Hindus, I tell them, "Your priests are not going to be happy to hear this" (notice how prudent I am this morning), "but God would be much happier, according to Jesus Christ, if you were transformed than if you worshipped. He would be much more pleased by your loving than by your adoration." And when I talk to Moslems, I say, "Your Ayatollah and your mullahs are not going to be happy to hear this, but God is going to be much more pleased by your being transformed into a loving person than by saying, "Lord, Lord." It's infinitely more important that you be waking up. That's spirituality, that's everything. If you have that, you have God. Then you worship "in spirit and in truth." When you become love, when you are transformed into love. The danger of what religion can do is very nicely brought out in a story told by Cardinal Martini, the Archbishop of Milan. The story has to do with an Italian couple that's getting married. They have an arrangement with the parish priest to have a little reception in the parish courtyard outside the church. But it rained, and they couldn't have the reception, so they said to the priest,

"Would it be all right if we had the celebration in the church?"

Now Father wasn't one bit happy about having a reception in the church, but they said, "We will eat a little cake, sing a little song, drink a little wine, and then go home." So Father was persuaded. But being good life-loving Italians they drank a little wine, sang a little song, then drank a little more wine, and sang some more songs, and within a half hour there was a great celebration going on in the church. And everybody was having a great time, lots of fun and frolic. But Father was all tense, pacing up and down in the sacristy, all upset about the noise they were making. The assistant pastor comes in and says, "I see you are quite tense".

"Of course, I'm tense. Listen to all the noise they are making, and in the House of God!, for heaven's sake!"

"Well, Father, they really had no place to go."

"I know that! But do they have to make all that racket?"

"Well, we mustn't forget, must we, Father, that Jesus himself was once present at a wedding!"

Father says, "I know Jesus Christ was present at a wedding banquet, *YOU* don't have to tell me Jesus Christ was present at a wedding banquet! But they didn't have the Blessed Sacrament there!!!"

You know there are times like that when the Blessed Sacrament becomes more important than Jesus Christ. When worship becomes more important than love, when the Church becomes more important than life. When God becomes more important than the neighbor. And so it goes on. That's the danger. To my mind this is what Jesus was evidently calling us to—first things first! The human being is much more important than the Sabbath. Doing what I tell you, namely, becoming what I am indicating to you, is much more important than Lord, Lord. But your mullah is not going to be happy to hear that, I assure you. Your priests are not going to be happy to hear that. Not generally. So that's what we have been talking about. Spirituality. Waking up. And as I told you, it is extremely important if you want to wake up to go in for what I call "self-observation." Be aware of what you're saying, be aware of what you're doing, be aware of what you're thinking, be aware of how you're acting. Be aware of where you're coming from, what your motives are. The unaware life is not worth living.

The unaware life is a mechanical life. It's not human, it's programmed, conditioned. We might as well be a stone, a block of wood. In the country where I come from, you have hundreds of thousands of people living in little hovels, in extreme poverty, who just manage to survive, working all day long, hard manual work, sleep and then wake up in the morning, eat something, and start all over again. And you sit back and think, "What a life." "Is that all that life holds in store for them?" And then you're suddenly jolted into the realization that 99.999% of people here are not much better. You can go to the movies, drive around in a car, you can go for a cruise. Do you think you are much better off than they are? You are just as dead as they are. Just as much a machine as they are—a slightly bigger one, but a machine nevertheless. That's sad. It's sad to think that people go through life like this.

People go through life with fixed ideas; they never change. They're just not aware of what's going on. They might as well be a block of wood, or a rock, a talking, walking, thinking machine. That's not human. They are puppets, jerked around by all kinds of things. Press a button and you get a reaction. You can almost predict how this person is going to react. If I study a person, I can tell you just how he or she is going to react. With my therapy group, sometimes I write on a piece of paper that so-and-so is going to start the session and so-and-so will reply. Do you think that's bad? Well, don't listen to people who say to you, "Forget yourself! Go out in love to others." Don't listen to them! They're all wrong. The worst thing you can do is forget yourself when you go out to others in the so-called helping attitude.

This was brought home to me very forcibly many years ago when I did my studies in psychology in Chicago. We had a course in counseling for priests. It was open only to priests who were actually engaged in counseling and who agreed to bring a taped session to class. There must have been about twenty of us. When it was my turn, I brought a cassette with an interview I had had with a young woman. The instructor put it in a recorder and we all began to listen to it. After five minutes, as was his custom, the instructor stopped the tape and asked, "Any comments?" Someone said to me, "Why did you ask her that question?" I said, "I'm not aware that I asked her a question. As a matter of fact,

I'm quite sure I did not ask any questions." He said, "You did." I was quite sure because at that time I was consciously following the method of Carl Rogers, which is person-oriented and nondirective. You don't ask questions and you don't interrupt or give advice. So I was very aware that I mustn't ask questions. Anyway, there was a dispute between us, so the instructor said, "Why don't we play the tape again?" So we played it again and there, to my horror, was a whopping big question, as tall as the Empire State Building, a huge question. The interesting thing to me was that I had heard that question three times, the first time, presumably, when I asked it, the second time when I listened to the tape in my room (because I wanted to take a good tape to class), and the third time when I heard it in the classroom. But it hadn't registered! I wasn't aware.

That happens frequently in my therapy sessions or in my spiritual direction. We tape-record the interview, and when the client listens to it, he or she says, "You know, I didn't really hear what you said during the interview. I only heard what you said when I listened to the tape." More interestingly, *I* didn't hear what *I* said during the interview. It's shocking to discover that I'm saying things in a therapy session that I'm not aware of. The full import of them only dawns on me later. Do you call that *human?* "Forget yourself and go out to others," you say! Anyhow, after we listened to the whole tape there in Chicago, the instructor said, "Are there any comments?" One of the priests, a fifty-year-old man to whom I had taken a liking, said to me, "Tony, I'd like to ask you a personal question. Would that be all right?" I said, "Yes, go ahead. If I don't want to answer it, I won't." He said, "Is this woman in the interview pretty?"

You know, honest to goodness, I was at a stage of my development (or undevelopment) where I didn't notice if someone was good-looking or not. It didn't matter to me. She was a sheep of Christ's flock; I was a pastor. I dispensed help. Isn't that great! It was the way we were trained. So I said to him, "What's that got to do with it?" He said, "Because you don't like her, do you?" I said, "What?!"

It hadn't ever struck me that I liked or disliked individuals. Like most people, I had an occasional dislike that would register in consciousness, but my attitude was mostly neutral. I asked, "What makes you say that?" He said, "The tape." We went through the tape again, and he said, "Listen to your voice. Notice how sweet it has become. You're irritated, aren't you?" I was, and I was only becoming aware of it right there. And what was I saying to her nondirectively? I was saying, "Don't come back." But I wasn't aware of that. My priest friend said, "She's a woman. She will have picked this up. When are you supposed to meet her next?" I said, "Next Wednesday." He said, "My guess is she won't come back." She didn't. I waited one week but she didn't come. I waited another week and she didn't come. Then I called her. I broke one of my rules: Don't be the rescuer.

I called her and said to her, "Remember that tape you allowed me to make for the class? It was a great help because the class pointed out all kinds of things to me" (I didn't tell her what!) "that would make the session somewhat more effective. So if you care to come back, that would make it more effective." She said, "All right, I'll come back." She did. The dislike was still there. It hadn't gone away, but it wasn't getting in the way. What you are aware of you are in control of; what you are not aware of is in control of you. You are always a slave to what you're not aware of. When you're aware of it, you're free from it. It's there, but you're not affected by it. You're not controlled by it; you're not enslaved by it. That's the difference.

Awareness, awareness, awareness, awareness. What they trained us to do in that course was to become participant observers. To put it somewhat graphically, I'd be talking to you and at the same time I'd be out there watching you and watching me. When I'm listening to you, it's infinitely more important for me to listen to me than to listen to you. Of course, it's important to listen to you, but it's more important that I listen to me. Otherwise I won't be hearing you. Or I'll be distorting everything you say. I'll be coming at you from my own conditioning. I'll be reacting to you in all kinds of ways from my insecurities, from my need to manipulate you, from my desire to succeed, from irritations and feelings that I might not be aware of. So it's frightfully important that I listen to me when I'm listening to you. That's what they were training us to do, obtaining awareness.

You don't always have to imagine yourself hovering somewhere in the air. Just to get a rough idea of what I'm talking about, imagine a good driver, driving a car, who's concentrating on what you're saying. In fact, he may even be having an argument with you, but he's perfectly aware of the road signals. The moment anything untoward happens, the moment there's any sound, or noise, or bump, he'll hear it at once. He'll say, "Are you sure you closed that door back there?" How did he do that? He was aware, he was alert. The focus of his attention was on the conversation, or argument, but his awareness was more diffused. He was taking in all kinds of things.

What I'm advocating here is not concentration. That's not important. Many meditative techniques inculcate concentration, but I'm leery of that. They involve violence and frequently they involve further programming and conditioning. What I would advocate is awareness, which is not the same as concentration at all. Concentration is a spotlight, a floodlight. You're open to anything that comes within the scope of your consciousness. You can be distracted from that, but when you're practicing awareness, you're never distracted. When awareness is turned on, there's never any distraction, because you're always aware of whatever happens to be.

Say I'm looking at those trees and I'm worrying. Am I distracted? I am distracted only if I mean to concentrate on the trees. But if I'm aware that I'm worried, too, that isn't a distraction at all. Just be aware of where your attention goes. When anything goes awry or anything untoward happens, you'll be alerted at once. Something's going wrong! The moment any negative feeling comes into consciousness, you'll be alerted. You're like the driver of the car.

I told you that St. Teresa of Avila said God gave her the grace of disidentifying herself with herself. You hear children talk that way. A two-year-old says, "Tommy had his breakfast this morning." He doesn't say "I," although he is Tommy. He says "Tommy"—in the third person. Mystics feel that way. They have disidentified from themselves and they are at peace.

This was the grace St. Teresa was talking about. This is the "I" that the mystic masters of the East are constantly urging people to discover. And those of the West, too! And you can count Meister Eckhart among them. They are urging people to discover the "I."

LABELS

The important thing is not to know who "I" is or what "I" is. You'll never succeed. There are no words for it. The important thing is to drop the labels. As the Japanese Zen masters say, "Don't seek the truth; just drop your opinions." Drop your theories; don't seek the truth. Truth isn't something you search for. If you stop being opinionated, you would know. Something similar happens here. If you drop your labels, you would know. What do I mean by labels? Every label you can conceive of except perhaps that of human being. I am a human being. Fair enough; doesn't say very much. But when you say, "I am successful," that's crazy. Success is not part of the "I." Success is something that comes and goes; it could be here today and gone to-morrow. That's not "I." When you said, "I was a success," you were in error; you were plunged into darkness. You identified yourself with success. The same thing when you said, "I am a failure, a lawyer, a businessman." You know what's going to happen to you if you identify yourself with these things. You're going to cling to them, you're going to be worried that they may fall apart, and that's where your suffering comes in. That is what I meant earlier when I said to you, "If you're suffering, you're asleep." Do you want a sign that you're asleep? Here it is: You're suffering. Suffering is a sign that you're out of touch with the truth. Suffering is given to you that you might open your eyes to the truth, that you might understand that there's falsehood somewhere, just as physical pain is given to you so you will understand that there is disease or illness somewhere. Suffering points out that there is falsehood somewhere. Suffering occurs when you clash with reality. When your illusions clash with reality, when your falsehoods clash with truth, then you have suffering. Otherwise there is no suffering.

OBSTACLES TO HAPPINESS

What I'm about to say will sound a bit pompous, but it's true. What is coming could be the most important minutes in your lives. If you could grasp this, you'd hit upon the secret of awakening. You would be happy forever. You would never be unhappy again. Nothing would have the power to hurt you again. I mean that, nothing. It's like when you throw black paint in the air; the air remains uncontaminated. You never color the air black. No matter what happens to you, you remain uncontaminated. You remain at peace. There are human beings who have attained this, what I call being human. Not this nonsense of being a puppet, jerked about this way and that way, letting events or other people tell you how to feel. So you proceed to feel it and you call it being vulnerable. Ha! I call it being a puppet. So you want to be a puppet? Press a button and you're down; do you like that? But if you refuse to identify with any of those labels, most of your worries cease.

Later we'll talk about fear of disease and death, but ordinarily you're worried about what's going to happen to your career. A small-time businessman, fifty-five years old, is sipping beer at a bar somewhere and he's saying, "Well, look at my classmates, they've really made it." The idiot! What does he mean, "They made it"? They've got their names in the newspaper. Do you call that making it? One is president of the corporation; the other has become the Chief Justice; somebody else has become this or that. Monkeys, all of them.

Who determines what it means to be a success? This stupid society! The main preoccupation of society is to keep society sick! And the sooner you realize that, the better. Sick, every one of them. They are loony, they're crazy. You became president of the lunatic asylum and you're proud of it even though it means nothing. Being president of a corporation has nothing to do with being a success in life. Having a lot of money has nothing to do with being a success in life. You're a success in life when you wake up! Then you don't have to apologize to anyone, you don't have to explain anything to anyone, you don't give a damn what anybody thinks about you or what anybody says about you. You have no worries; you're happy. That's what I call being a success. Having a good job or being famous or having a great reputation has absolutely nothing to do with happiness or success. Nothing! It is totally irrevelant. All he's really worried about is what his children will think about him, what the neighbors will think about him, what his wife will think about him. He should have become famous. Our society and culture drill that into our heads day and night. People who made it! Made what?! Made asses of themselves. Because they drained all their energy getting something that was worthless. They're frightened and confused, they are puppets like the rest. Look at them strutting across the stage. Look how upset they get if they have a stain on their shirt. Do you call that a success? Look at how frightened they are at the prospect they might not be reelected. Do you call that a success? They are controlled, so manipulated. They are unhappy people, they are miserable people. They don't enjoy life. They are constantly tense and anxious. Do you call that human? And do you know why that happens? Only one reason: They identified with some label. They identified the "I" with their money or their job or their profession. That was their error.

Did you hear about the lawyer who was presented with a

plumber's bill? He said to the plumber, "Hey, you're charging me two hundred dollars an hour. I don't make that kind of money as a lawyer." The plumber said, "I didn't make that kind of money when I was a lawyer either!" You could be a plumber or a lawyer or a businessman or a priest, but that does not affect the essential "I". It doesn't affect you. If I change my profession tomorrow, it's just like changing my clothes. I am untouched. *Are* you your clothes? *Are* you your name? *Are* you your profession? Stop identifying with them. They come and go.

When you really understand this, no criticism can affect you. No flattery or praise can affect you either. When someone says, "You're a great guy," what is he talking about? He's talking about "me," he's not talking about "I." "I" is neither great nor small. "I" is neither successful nor a failure. It is none of these labels. These things come and go. These things depend on the criteria society establishes. These things depend on your conditioning. These things depend on the mood of the person who happens to be talking to you right now. It has nothing to do with "I." "I" is none of these labels. "Me" is generally selfish, foolish, childish—a great big ass. So when you say, "You're an ass," I've known it for years! The conditioned self—what did you expect? I've known it for years. Why do you identify with him? Silly! That isn't "I," that's "me."

Do you want to be happy? Uninterrupted happiness is uncaused. True happiness is uncaused. You cannot make me happy. You are not my happiness. You say to the awakened person, "Why are you happy?" and the awakened person replies, "Why not?"

Happiness is our natural state. Happiness is the natural state of little children, to whom the kingdom belongs until they have been polluted and contaminated by the stupidity of society and culture. To acquire happiness you don't have to do anything, because happiness cannot be acquired. Does anybody know why? Because we have it already. How can you acquire what you already have? Then why don't you experience it? Because you've got to drop something. You've got to drop illusions. You don't have to add any-thing in order to be happy; you've got to drop something. Life is easy, life is delightful. It's only hard on your illu-sions, your ambitions, your greed, your cravings. Do you know where these things come from? From having identi-fied with all kinds of labels!

FOUR STEPS TO WISDOM

The first thing you need to do is get in touch with nega-tive feelings that you're not even aware of. Lots of people have negative feelings they're not aware of. Lots of people are depressed and they're not aware they are depressed. It's only when they make contact with joy that they understand how depressed they were. You can't deal with a cancer that you haven't detected. You can't get rid of boll weevils on your farm if you're not aware of their existence. The first thing you need is awareness of your negative feelings. What negative feelings? Gloominess, for instance. You're feeling gloomy and moody. You feel self-hatred or guilt. You feel that life is pointless, that it makes no sense; you've got hurt feelings, you're feeling nervous and tense. Get in touch with those feelings first.

The second step (this is a four-step program) is to understand that the feeling is in you, not in reality. That's such a self-evident thing, but do you think people know it? They don't, believe mc. They've got Ph.D.s and are presidents of universities, but they haven't understood this. They didn't teach me how to live at school. They taught me everything else. As one man said, "I got a pretty good education. It took me years to get over it." That's what spirituality is all about, you know: unlearning. Unlearning all the rubbish they taught you.

Negative feelings are in you, not in reality. So stop trying to change reality. That's crazy! Stop trying to change the other person. We spend all our time and energy trying to change external circumstances, trying to change our spouses, our bosses, our friends, our enemies, and everybody else. We don't have to change anything. Negative feelings are in *you*. No person on earth has the power to make you unhappy. There is no event on earth that has the power to disturb you or hurt you. No event, condition, situation, or person. Nobody told you this; they told you the opposite. That's why you're in the mess that you're in right now. That is why you're asleep. They never told you this. But it's self-evident.

Let's suppose that rain washes out a picnic. Who is feeling negative? The rain? Or *you?* What's causing the negative feeling? The rain or your reaction? When you bump your knee against a table, the table's fine. It's busy being what it was made to be—a table. The pain is in your knee, not in the table. The mystics keep trying to tell us that reality is all right. Reality is not problematic. Problems exist only in the human mind. We might add: in the stupid, sleeping human mind. Reality is not problematic. Take away human beings from this planet and life would go on, nature would go on in all its loveliness and violence. Where would the problem be? No problem. You created the problem. You are the problem. You identified with "me" and that is the problem. The feeling is in you, not in reality.

The third step: Never identify with that feeling. It has nothing to do with the "I." Don't define your essential self in terms of that feeling. Don't say, "I am depressed." If you want to say, "It is depressed," that's all right. If you want to say depression is there, that's fine; if you want to say gloominess is there, that's fine. But not: I am gloomy. You're defining yourself in terms of the feeling. That's your illusion; that's your mistake. There is a depression there right now, there are hurt feelings there right now, but let it be, leave it alone. It will pass. Everything passes, everything. Your depressions and your thrills have nothing to do with happiness. Those are the swings of the pendulum. If you seek kicks or thrills, get ready for depression. Do you want your drug? Get ready for the hangover. One end of the pendulum swings to the other.

This has nothing to do with "I"; it has nothing to do with happiness. It is the "me." If you remember this, if you say it to yourself a thousand times, if you try these three steps a thousand times, you will get it. You might not need to do it even three times. I don't know; there's no rule for it. But do it a thousand times and you'll make the biggest discovery in your life. To hell with those gold mines in Alaska. What are you going to do with that gold? If you're not happy, you can't live. So you found gold. What does that matter? You're a king; you're a princess. You're free; you don't care anymore about being accepted or rejected, that makes no difference. Psychologists tell us how important it is to get a sense of belonging. Baloney! Why do you want to belong to anybody? It doesn't matter anymore.

A friend of mine told me that there's an African tribe where capital punishment consists of being ostracized. If you were kicked out of New York, or wherever you're residing, you wouldn't die. How is it that the African tribesman died? Because he partakes of the common stupidity of humanity. He thinks he will not be able to live if he does not belong. It's very different from most people, or is it? He's convinced he needs to belong. But you don't need to belong to anybody or anything or any group. You don't even need to be in love. Who told you you do? What you need is to be free. What you need is to love. That's it; that's your nature. But what you're really telling me is that you want to be desired. You want to be applauded, to be attractive, to have all the little monkeys running after you.

You're wasting your life. *Wake up!* You don't need this. You can be blissfully happy without it.

Your society is not going to be happy to hear this, because you become terrifying when you open your eyes and understand this. How do you control a person like this? He doesn't need you; he's not threatened by your criticism; he doesn't care what you think of him or what you say about him. He's cut all those strings; he's not a puppet any longer. It's terrifying. "So we've got to get rid of him. He tells the truth; he has become fearless; he has stopped being human." *Human!* Behold! A human being at last! He broke out of his slavery, broke out of their prison.

No event justifies a negative feeling. There is no situation in the world that justifies a negative feeling. That's what all our mystics have been crying themselves hoarse to tell us. But nobody listens. The negative feeling is in you. In the Bhagavad-Gita, the sacred book of the Hindus, Lord Krishna says to Arjuna, "Plunge into the heat of battle and keep your heart at the lotus feet of the Lord." A marvelous sentence.

You don't have to do anything to acquire happiness. The great Meister Eckhart said very beautifully, "God is not attained by a process of addition to anything in the soul, but by a process of subtraction." You don't do anything to be free, you drop something. Then you're free.

It reminds me of the Irish prisoner who dug a tunnel under the prison wall and managed to escape. He comes out right in the middle of a school playground where little children are playing. Of course, when he emerges from the tunnel he can't restrain himself anymore and begins to jump up and down, crying, "I'm free, I'm free, I'm free! A little girl there looks at him scornfully and says, "That's nothing. I'm four."

The fourth step: How do you change things? How do you change yourselves? There are many things you must understand here, or rather, just one thing that can be expressed in many ways. Imagine a patient who goes to a doctor and tells him what he is suffering from. The doctor says, "Very well, I've understood your symptoms. Do you know what I will do? I will prescribe a medicine for your neighbor!" The patient replies, "Thank you very much, Doctor, that makes me feel much better." Isn't that absurd? But that's what we all do. The person who is asleep always thinks he'll feel better if somebody else changes. You're suffering because you are asleep, but you're thinking, "How wonderful life would be if somebody else would change; how wonderful life would be if my neighbor changed, my wife changed, my boss changed."

We always want someone else to change so that we will feel good. But has it ever struck you that even if your wife changes or your husband changes, what does that do to you? You're just as vulnerable as before; you're just as idiotic as before; you're just as asleep as before. You are the one who needs to change, who needs to take medicine. You keep insisting, "I feel good because the world is right." *Wrong!* The world is right because I feel good. That's what all the mystics are saying.

ALL'S RIGHT WITH THE WORLD

When you awaken, when you understand, when you see, the world becomes right. We're always bothered by the problem of evil. There's a powerful story about a little boy walking along the bank of a river. He sees a crocodile who is trapped in a net. The crocodile says, "Would you have pity on me and release me? I may look ugly, but it isn't my fault, you know. I was made this way. But whatever my external appearance, I have a mother's heart. I came this morning in search of food for my young ones and got caught in this trap!" So the boy says, "Ah, if I were to help you out of that trap, you'd grab me and kill me." The crocodile asks, "Do you think I would do that to my bene-factor and liberator?" So the boy is persuaded to take the net off and the crocodile grabs him. As he is being forced between the jaws of the crocodile, he says, "So this is what I get for my good actions." And the crocodile says, "Well, don't take it personally, son, this is the way the world is, this is the law of life." The boy disputes this, so the croco-dile says, "Do you want to ask someone if it isn't so?" The boys sees a bird sitting on a branch and says, "Bird, is what the crocodile says right?" The bird says, "The crocodile is right. Look at me. I was coming home one day with food for my fledglings. Imagine my horror to see a snake crawl-ing up the tree, making straight for my nest. I was totally helpless. It kept devouring my young ones, one after the other. I kept screaming and shouting, but it was useless. The crocodile is right, this is the law of life, this is the way the world is." "See," says the crocodile. But the boy says, "Let me ask someone else." So the crocodile says, "Well, all right, go ahead." There was an old donkey passing by on the bank of the river. "Donkey," says the boy, "this is what the crocodile says. Is the crocodile right?" The donkey says, "The crocodile is quite right. Look at me. I've worked and slaved for my master all my life and he barely gave me enough to eat. Now that I'm old and useless, he has turned me loose, and here I am wandering in the jungle, waiting for some wild beast to pounce on me and put an end to my life. The crocodile is right, this is the law of life, this is the way the world is." "See," says the crocodile. "Let's go!" The boy says, "Give me one more chance, one last chance. Let me ask one other being. Remember how good I was to you?" So the crocodile says, "All right, your last chance." The boy sees a rabbit passing by, and he says, "Rabbit, is the crocodile right?" The rabbit sits on his haunches and says to the crocodile, "Did you say that to that boy? The crocodile says, "Yes, I did." "Wait a minute," says the rabbit. "We've got to discuss this." "Yes," says the crocodile. But the rabbit says, "How can we discuss it when you've got that boy in your mouth? Release him; he's got to take part in the discussion, too." The crocodile says, "You're a clever one, you are. The moment I release him, he'll run away." The rabbit says, "I thought you had more sense than that. If he attempted to run away, one slash of your tail would kill him." "Fair enough," says the crocodile, and he released the boy. The moment the boy is released, the rabbit says, "Run!" And the boy runs and escapes. Then the rabbit says

to the boy, "Don't you enjoy crocodile flesh? Wouldn't the
people in your village like a good meal? You didn't really
release that crocodile; most of his body is still caught in that
net. Why don't you go to the village and bring everybody
and have a banquet." That's exactly what the boy does. He
goes to the village and calls all the menfolk. They come
with their axes and staves and spears and kill the crocodile.
The boy's dog comes, too, and when the dog sees the rabbit,
he gives chase, catches hold of the rabbit, and throttles him.
The boy comes on the scene too late, and as he watches the
rabbit die, he says, "The crocodile was right, this is the way
the world is, this is the law of life."

There is no explanation you can give that would explain
away all the sufferings and evil and torture and destruction
and hunger in the world! You'll never explain it. You can
try gamely with your formulas, religious and otherwise, but
you'll never explain it. Because life is a mystery, which
means your thinking mind cannot make sense out of it. For
that you've got to wake up and then you'll suddenly realize
that reality is not problematic, you are the problem.

❦

SLEEPWALKING

The scriptures are always hinting of that, but you'll never
understand a word of what the scriptures are saying until
you wake up. Sleeping people read the scriptures and cru-
cify the Messiah on the basis of them. You've got to wake

up to make sense out of the scriptures. When you do wake up, they make sense. So does reality. But you'll never be able to put it into words. You'd rather do something? But even there we've got to make sure that you're not swinging into action simply to get rid of your negative feelings. Many people swing into action only to make things worse. They're not coming from love, they're coming from negative feelings. They're coming from guilt, anger, hate; from a sense of injustice or whatever. You've got to make sure of your "being" before you swing into action. You have to make sure of who you are before you act. Unfortunately, when sleeping people swing into action, they simply substitute one cruelty for another, one injustice for another. And so it goes. Meister Eckhart says, "It is not by your actions that you will be saved" (or awakened; call it by any word you want), "but by your being. It is not by what you do, but by what you are that you will be judged." What good is it to you to feed the hungry, give the thirsty to drink, or visit prisoners in jail?

Remember that sentence from Paul: "If I give my body to be burned and all my goods to feed the poor and have not love . . ." It's not your actions, it's your being that counts. *Then* you might swing into action. You might or might not. You can't decide that until you're awake. Unfortunately, all the emphasis is concentrated on changing the world and very little emphasis is given to waking up. When you wake up, you will know what to do or what not to do. Some mystics are very strange, you know. Like Jesus, who said something like "I wasn't sent to those people; I limit myself to what I am supposed to do right now. Later, maybe." Some mystics go silent. Mysteriously, some of them sing songs. Some of them are into service. We're never sure. They're a law unto themselves; they know exactly what is to be done. "Plunge into the heat of battle and keep your heart at the lotus feet of the Lord," as I said to you earlier.

Imagine that you're unwell and in a foul mood, and they're taking you through some lovely countryside. The landscape is beautiful but you're not in the mood to see anything. A few days later you pass the same place and you say, "Good heavens, where was I that I didn't notice all of this?" Everything becomes beautiful when you change. Or you look at the trees and the mountains through windows that are wet with rain from a storm, and everything looks blurred and shapeless. You want to go right out there and change those trees, change those mountains. Wait a minute, let's examine your window. When the storm ceases and the rain stops, and you look out the window, you say, "Well, how different everything looks." We see people and things not as they are, but as we are. That is why when two people look at something or someone, you get two different reactions. We see things and people not as they are, but as we are.

Remember that sentence from scripture about everything turning into good for those who love God? When you finally awake, you don't try to make good things happen; they just happen. You understand suddenly that everything that happens to you is good. Think of some people you're living with whom you want to change. You find them moody, inconsiderate, unreliable, treacherous, or whatever. But when you are different, they'll be different. That's an infallible and miraculous cure. The day you are different, they will become different. And you will see them differently, too. Someone who seemed terrifying will now seem frightened. Someone who seemed rude will seem frightened. All of a sudden, no one has the power to hurt you anymore. No one has the power to put pressure on you. It's something like this: You leave a book on the table and I pick it up and say, "You're pressing this book on me. I have to pick it up or not pick it up." People are so busy accusing everyone else, blaming everyone else, blaming life, blaming society, blaming their neighbor. You'll never change that way; you'll continue in your nightmare, you'll never wake up.

Put this program into action, a thousand times: (a) identify the negative feelings in you; (b) understand that they are in you, not in the world, not in external reality; (c) do not see them as an essential part of "I"; these things come and go; (d) understand that when you change, everything changes.

CHANGE AS GREED

That still leaves us with a big question: Do I do anything to change myself?

I've got a big surprise for you, lots of good news! You don't have to do anything. The more you do, the worse it gets. All you have to do is understand.

Think of somebody you are living with or working with whom you do not like, who causes negative feelings to arise in you. Let's help you to understand what's going on. The first thing you need to understand is that the negative feeling is inside you. You are responsible for the negative feeling, not the other person. Someone else in your place would be perfectly calm and at ease in the presence of this person; they wouldn't be affected. *You* are. Now, understand another thing, that you're making a demand. You have an expectation of this person. Can you get in touch with that? Then say to this person, "I have no right to make any demands on you." In saying that, you will drop your expectation. "I have no right to make any demands on you. Oh, I'll protect myself from the consequences of your actions or your moods or whatever, but you can go right ahead and be what you choose to be. I have no right to make any demands on you."

See what happens to you when you do this. If there's a resistance to saying it, my, how much you're going to discover about your "me." Let the dictator in you come out, let the tyrant come out. You thought you were such a little lamb, didn't you? But I'm a tyrant and you're a tyrant. A little variation on "I'm an ass, you're an ass." I'm a dictator, you're a dictator. I want to run your life for you; I want to tell you exactly how you're expected to be and how you're expected to behave, and you'd better behave as I have decided or I shall punish myself by having negative feelings. Remember what I told you, everybody's a lunatic.

A woman told me her son had gotten an award at his high school. It was for excellence in sports and academics. She was happy for him, but was almost tempted to say to him, "Don't glory in that award, because it's setting you up for the time when you can't perform as well." She was in a dilemma: how to prevent his future disillusionment without bursting his bubble now.

Hopefully, he'll learn as she herself grows in wisdom. It's not a matter of anything she says to him. It's something that eventually she will become. Then she will understand. Then she will know what to say and when to say it. That award was a result of competition, which can be cruel if it is built on hatred of oneself and of others. People get a good feeling on the basis of somebody getting a bad feeling; you win *over* somebody else. Isn't that terrible? Taken for granted in a lunatic asylum!

There's an American doctor who wrote about the effect of competition on his life. He went to medical school in Switzerland and there was a fairly large contingent of Americans at that school. He said some of the students went into shock when they realized that there were no grades, there were no awards, there was no dean's list, no first or second in the class at the school. You either passed or you didn't. He said, "Some of us just couldn't take it. We became almost paranoid. We thought there must be some kind of trick here." So some of them went to another school. Those who survived suddenly discovered a strange thing they had never noticed at American universities: students, brilliant ones, helping others to pass, sharing notes. His son goes to medical school in the United States and he tells him that, in the lab, people often tamper with the microscope so that it'll take the next student three or four minutes to readjust it. Competition. They have to succeed, they have to be perfect. And he tells a lovely little story which he says is factual, but it could also serve as a beautiful parable. There was a little town in America where people gathered in the evening to make music. They had a saxophonist, a drummer, and a violinist, mostly old people. They got together for the company and for the sheer joy of making music, though they didn't do it very well. So they were enjoying themselves, having a great time, until one day they decided to get a new conductor who had a lot of ambition and drive. The new conductor told them, "Hey, folks, we have to have a concert; we have to prepare a concert for the town." Then he gradually got rid of some people who didn't play too well, hired a few professional musicians, got an orchestra into shape, and they all got their names in the newspapers. Wasn't that wonderful? So they decided to move to the big city and play there. But some of the old people had tears in their eyes, they said, "It was so wonderful in the old days when we did things badly and enjoyed them." So cruelty came into their lives, but nobody recognized it as cruelty. See how lunatic people have become!

Some of you ask me what I meant when I said, "You go ahead and be yourself, that's all right, but I'll protect myself, I'll be myself." In other words, I won't allow you to manipulate me. I'll live my life; I'll go my own way; I'll keep myself free to think my thoughts, to follow my inclinations and tastes. And I'll say no to you. If I feel I don't want to be in your company, it won't be because of any negative feelings you cause in me. Because you don't anymore. You don't have any more power over me. I simply might prefer other people's company. So when you say to me, "How about a movie tonight?" I'll say, "Sorry, I want to go with someone else; I enjoy his company more than yours." And that's all right. To say no to people—that's wonderful; that's part of waking up. Part of waking up is that you live your life as you see fit. And understand: That is *not* selfish. The selfish thing is to demand that someone else live their life as YOU see fit. *That's* selfish. It is not selfish to live your life as you see fit. The selfishness lies in demanding that someone else live their life to suit your tastes, or your pride, or your profit, or your pleasure. That is truly selfish. So I'll protect myself. I won't feel obligated to be with you; I won't feel obligated to say yes to you. If I find your company pleasant, then I'll enjoy it without clinging to it. But I no longer avoid you because of any negative feelings you create in me. You don't have that power anymore.

Awakening should be a surprise. When you don't expect something to happen and it happens, you feel surprise. When Webster's wife caught him kissing the maid, she told him she was very surprised. Now, Webster was a stickler for using words accurately (understandably, since he wrote a dictionary), so he answered her, "No, my dear, I am surprised. You are astonished!"

Some people make awakening a goal. They are determined to get there; they say, "I refuse to be happy until I'm awakened." In that case, it's better to be the way you are, simply to be aware of the way you are. Simple awareness is happiness compared with trying to react all the time. People react so quickly because they are not aware. You will come to understand that there are times when you will inevitably react, even in awareness. But as awareness grows, you react less and act more. It really doesn't matter.

There's a story of a disciple who told his guru that he was going to a far place to meditate and hopefully attain enlightenment. So he sent the guru a note every six months to report the progress he was making. The first report said, "Now I understand what it means to lose the self." The guru tore up the note and threw it in the wastepaper basket. After six months he got another report, which said, "Now I have attained sensitivity to all beings." He tore it up. Then a third report said, "Now I understand the secret of the one and the many." It too was torn up. And so it went on for years, until finally no reports came in. After a time the guru became curious and one day there was a traveler going to that far place. The guru said, "Why don't you find out what happened to that fellow." Finally, he got a note from his disciple. It said, "What does it matter?" And when the guru read that, he said, "He made it! He made it! He finally got it! He got it!"

And there is the story about a soldier on the battlefield who would simply drop his rifle to the ground, pick up a scrap of paper lying there, and look at it. Then he would let it flutter from his hands to the ground. And then he'd move somewhere else and do the same thing. So others said, "This man is exposing himself to death. He needs help." So they put him in the hospital and got the best psychiatrist to work on him. But it seemed to have no effect. He wandered around the wards picking up scraps of paper, looking at them idly, and letting them flutter to the ground. In the end they said, "We've got to discharge this man from the army." So they call him in and give him a discharge certificate and he idly picks it up, looks at it, and shouts, "This is it? This is it." He finally got it.

So begin to be aware of your present condition whatever that condition is. Stop being a dictator. Stop trying to push yourself somewhere. Then someday you will understand that simply by awareness you have already attained what you were pushing yourself toward.

❦
A CHANGED PERSON

In your pursuit of awareness, don't make demands. It's more like obeying the traffic rules. If you don't observe traffic rules, you pay the penalty. Here in the United States you drive on the right side of the road; in England you drive on the left; in India you drive on the left. If you don't, you pay the penalty; there is no room for hurt feelings or demands or expectations; you just abide by the traffic rules.

You ask where compassion comes in, where guilt comes in in all this. You'll know when you're awake. If you're feeling guilty right now, how on earth can I explain it to you? How would you know what compassion is? You know, sometimes people want to imitate Christ, but when a monkey plays a saxophone, that doesn't make him a musician. You can't imitate Christ by imitating his external behavior. You've got to be Christ. Then you'll know exactly what to do in a particular situation, given your temperament, your character, and the character and temperament of the person you're dealing with. No one has to tell you. But to do that, you must *be* what Christ was. An external imitation will get you nowhere. If you think that compassion implies softness, there's no way I can describe compassion to you, absolutely no way, because compassion can be very hard. Compassion can be very rude, compassion can jolt you, compassion can roll up its sleeves and operate on you. Compassion is all kinds of things. Compassion can be very soft, but there's no way of knowing that. It's only when you become love—in other words, when you have dropped your illusions and attachments—that you will "know."

As you identify less and less with the "I," you will be more at ease with everybody and with everything. Do you know why? Because you are no longer afraid of being hurt or not liked. You no longer desire to impress anyone. Can you imagine the relief when you don't have to impress anybody anymore? Oh, what a relief. Happiness at last! You no longer feel the need or the compulsion to explain things anymore. It's all right. What is there to be explained? And you don't feel the need or compulsion to apologize anymore. I'd much rather hear you say, "I've come awake," than hear you say, "I'm sorry." I'd much rather hear you say to me, "I've come awake since we last met; what I did to you won't happen again," than to hear you say, "I'm so sorry for what I did to you." Why would anyone demand an apology? You have something to explore in that. Even when someone supposedly was mean to you, there is no room for apology.

Nobody was mean to you. Somebody was mean to what he or she thought was you, but not to you. Nobody ever rejects you; they're only rejecting what they think you are. But that cuts both ways. Nobody ever accepts you either. Until people come awake, they are simply accepting or rejecting their image of you. They've fashioned an image of you, and they're rejecting or accepting that. See how devastating it is to go deeply into that. It's a bit too liberating. But how easy it is to love people when you understand this. How easy it is to love everyone when you don't identify with what they imagine you are or they are. It becomes easy to love them, to love everybody.

I observe "me," but I do not think about "me." Because the thinking "me" does a lot of bad thinking, too. But when I watch "me," I am constantly aware that this is a reflection. In reality, you don't really think of "I" and "me." You're like a person driving the car; he doesn't ever want to lose consciousness of the car. It's all right to daydream, but not to lose consciousness of your surroundings. You must always be alert. It's like a mother sleeping; she doesn't hear the planes roaring above the house, but she hears the slightest whimper of her baby. She's alert, she's awake in that sense. One cannot say anything about the awakened state; one can only talk about the sleeping state. One hints at the awakened state. One cannot say anything about happiness. Happiness cannot be defined. What can be defined is misery. Drop unhappiness and you will know. Love cannot be defined; unlove can. Drop unlove, drop fear, and you will know. We want to find out what the awakened person is like. But you'll know only when you get there.

Am I implying, for example, that we shouldn't make demands on our children? What I said was: "You don't have a right to make any demands." Sooner or later that child is going to have to get rid of you, in keeping with the injunction of the Lord. And you're going to have no rights over him at all. In fact, he really isn't your child and he never was. He belongs to life, not to you. No one belongs to you. What you're talking about is a child's education. If you want lunch, you better come in between twelve and one or you don't get lunch. Period. That's the way things are run here. You don't come on time, you don't get your lunch. You're free, that true, but you must take the consequences.

When I talk about not having expectations of others, or

not making demands on them, I mean expectations and demands for my well-being. The President of the United
States obviously has to make demands on people. The traffic
policeman obviously has to make demands on people. But
these are demands on their behavior—traffic laws, good or-
ganization, the smooth running of society. They are not
intended to make the President or traffic policeman feel
good.

ARRIVING AT SILENCE

Everyone asks me about what will happen when they finally arrive. Is this just curiosity? We're always asking how
would this fit into that system, or whether this would make
sense in that context, or what it will feel like when we get
there. Get started and you will know; it cannot be described. It is said widely in the East, "Those who know, do
not say; those who say, do not know." It cannot be said;
only the opposite can be said. The guru cannot give you the
truth. Truth cannot be put into words, into a formula. That
isn't the truth. That isn't reality. Reality cannot be put into
a formula. The guru can only point out your errors. When
you drop your errors, you will know the truth. And even
then you cannot say. This is common teaching among the
great Catholic mystics. The great Thomas Aquinas, toward
the end of his life, wouldn't write and wouldn't talk; he had
seen. I had thought he kept that famous silence of his for

only a couple of months, but it went on for years. He realized he had made a fool of himself, and he said so explicitly. It's as if you had never tasted a green mango and you ask me, "What does it taste like?" I'd say to you, "Sour," but in giving you a word, I've put you off the track. Try to understand that. Most people aren't very wise; they seize upon the word—upon the words of scripture, for example—and they get it all wrong. "Sour," I say, and you ask, "Sour like vinegar, sour like a lemon?" No, not sour like a lemon, but sour like a mango. "But I never tasted one," you say. Too bad! But you go ahead and write a doctoral thesis on it. You wouldn't have if you had tasted it. You really wouldn't. You'd have written a doctoral thesis on other things, but not on mangoes. And the day you finally taste a green mango, you say, "God, I made a fool of myself. I shouldn't have written that thesis." That's exactly what Thomas Aquinas did.

A great German philosopher and theologian wrote a whole book specifically on the silence of St. Thomas. He simply went silent. Wouldn't talk. In the prologue of his *Summa Theologica,* which was the summary of all his theology, he says, "About God, we cannot say what He is but rather what He is not. And so we cannot speak about how He is but rather how He is not." And in his famous commentary on Boethius' *De Sancta Trinitate* he says there are three ways of knowing God: (1) in the creation, (2) in God's actions through history, and (3) in the highest form of the knowledge of God—to know God *tamquam ignotum* (to know God as the unknown). The highest form of talking about the Trinity is to know that one does not know. Now, this is not an Oriental Zen master speaking. This is a canonized saint of the Roman Catholic Church, the prince of theologians for centuries. To know God as unknown. In another place St. Thomas even says: as unknowable. Reality, God, divinity, truth, love are unknowable; that means they cannot be comprehended by the thinking mind. That would set at rest so many questions people have because we're always living under the illusion that we know. We don't. We cannot know.

What is scripture, then? It's a hint, a clue, not a description. The fanaticism of one sincere believer who thinks he knows causes more evil than the united efforts of two hundred rogues. It's terrifying to see what sincere believers will do because they think they know. Wouldn't it be wonderful if we had a world where everybody said, "We don't know"? One big barrier dropped. Wouldn't that be marvelous?

A man born blind comes to me and asks, "What is this thing called green?" How does one describe the color green to someone who was born blind? One uses analogies. So I say, "The color green is something like soft music." "Oh," he says, "like soft music." "Yes," I say, "soothing and soft music." So a second blind man comes to me and asks, "What is the color green?" I tell him it's something like soft satin, very soft and soothing to the touch. So the next day I notice that the two blind men are bashing each other over the head with bottles. One is saying, "It's soft like music"; the other is saying, "It's soft like satin." And on it goes.

Neither of them knows what they're talking about, because if they did, they'd shut up. It's as bad as that. It's even worse, because one day, say, you give sight to this blind man, and he's sitting there in the garden and he's looking all around him, and you say to him, "Well, now you know what the color green is." And he answers, "That's true. I heard some of it this morning!"

The fact is that you're surrounded by God and you don't see God, because you "know" about God. The final barrier to the vision of God is your God concept. You miss God because you think you know. That's the terrible thing about religion. That's what the gospels were saying, that religious people "knew," so they got rid of Jesus. The highest knowledge of God is to know God as unknowable. There is far too much God talk; the world is sick of it. There is too little awareness, too little love, too little happiness, but let's not use those words either. There's too little dropping of illusions, dropping of errors, dropping of attachments and cruelty, too little awareness. That's what the world is suffering from, not from a lack of religion. Religion is supposed to be about a lack of awareness, of waking up. Look what we've degenerated into. Come to my country and see them killing one another over religion. You'll find it everywhere. "The one who knows, does not say; the one who says, does not know." All revelations, however divine, are never any more than a finger pointing to the moon. As we say in the East, "When the sage points to the moon, all the idiot sees is the finger."

Jean Guiton, a very pious and orthodox French writer,

adds a terrifying comment: "We often use the finger to gouge eyes out." Isn't that terrible? Awareness, awareness, awareness! In awareness is healing; in awareness is truth; in awareness is salvation; in awareness is spirituality; in awareness is growth; in awareness is love; in awareness is awakening. Awareness.

I need to talk about words and concepts because I must explain to you why it is, when we look at a tree, we really don't see. We *think* we do, but we don't. When we look at a person, we really don't see that person, we only think we do. What we're seeing is something that we fixed in our mind. We get an impression and we hold on to that impression, and we keep looking at a person through that impression. And we do this with almost everything. If you understand that, you will understand the loveliness and beauty of being aware of everything around you. Because reality is there; "God," whatever that is, is there. It's all *there*. The poor little fish in the ocean says, "Excuse me, I'm looking for the ocean. Can you tell me where I can find it?" Pathetic, isn't it? If we would just open our eyes and see, then we would understand.

LOSING *THE RAT RACE*

Let's get back to that marvelous sentence in the gospel about losing oneself in order to find oneself. One finds it in most religious literature and in all religious and spiritual and mystical literature.

How does one lose oneself? Did you ever *try* to lose something? That's right, the harder you try, the harder it gets. It's when you're not trying that you lose things. You lose something when you're not aware. Well, how does one die to oneself? We're talking about death now, we're not talking about suicide. We're not told to kill the self, but to die. Causing pain to the self, causing suffering to the self would be self-defeating. It would be counterproductive. You're never so full of yourself as when you're in pain. You're never so centered on yourself as when you're depressed. You're never so ready to forget yourself as when you are happy. Happiness releases you from self. It is suffering and pain and misery and depression that tie you to the self. Look how conscious you are of your tooth when you have a toothache. When you don't have a toothache, you're not even aware you have a tooth, or that you have a head, for that matter, when you don't have a headache. But it's so different when you have a splitting headache.

So it's quite false, quite erroneous, to think that the way to deny the self is to cause pain to the self, to go in for abnegation, mortification, as these were traditionally understood. To deny the self, to die to it, to lose it, is to understand its true nature. When you do that, it will disappear; it will vanish. Suppose somebody walks into my room one day. I say, "Come right in. May I know who you are?" And he says, "I am Napoleon." And I say, "Not the Napoleon . . ." And he says, "Precisely. Bonaparte, Emperor of France." "What do you know!" I say, even while I'm thinking to myself, "I better handle this guy with care."

"Sit down, Your Majesty," I say. "Well, they tell me you're a pretty good spiritual director. I have a spiritual problem. I'm anxious, I'm finding it hard to trust in God. I have my armies in Russia, see, and I'm spending sleepless nights wondering how it's going to turn out." So I say, "Well, Your Majesty, I could certainly prescribe something for that. What I suggest is that you read chapter 6 of Matthew: "Consider the lilies of the field . . . they neither toil nor spin."

By this point I'm wondering who is crazier, this guy or me. But I go along with this lunatic. That's what the wise guru does with you in the beginning. He goes along with you; he takes your troubles seriously. He'll wipe a tear or two from your eye. You're crazy, but you don't know it yet. The time has to come soon when he'll pull the rug out from under your feet and tell you, "Get off it, you're not Napoleon." In those famous dialogues of St. Catherine of Siena, God is reported to have said to her, "I am He who is; you are she who is not." Have you ever experienced your is–not-ness? In the East we have an image for this. It is the image of the dancer and the dance. God is viewed as the dancer and creation as God's dance. It isn't as if God is the big dancer and you are the little dancer. Oh no. You're not a dancer at all. You are *being* danced! Did you ever experience that? So when the man comes to his senses and realizes that he is not Napoleon, he does not cease to be. He continues to be, but he suddenly realizes that he is something other than what he thought he was.

To lose the self is to suddenly realize that you are something other than what you thought you were. You thought you were at the center; now you experience yourself as satellite. You thought you were the dancer; you now experience yourself as the dance. These are just analogies, images, so you cannot take them literally. They just give you a clue, a hint; they're only pointers, don't forget. So you cannot press them too much. Don't take them too literally.

PERMANENT WORTH

To move on to another idea, there is the whole matter of one's personal worth. Personal worth doesn't mean self-worth. Where do you get self-worth from? Do you get it from success in your work? Do you get it from having a lot of money? Do you get it from attracting a lot of men (if you're a woman) or a lot of women (if you're a man)? How fragile all that is, how transitory. When we talk about self-worth, are we not talking, really, about how we are reflected in the mirrors of other people's minds? But do we need to depend on that? One understands one's personal worth when one no longer identifies or defines one's self in terms of these transient things. I'm not beautiful because everyone says I'm beautiful. I'm really neither beautiful nor ugly. These are things that come and go. I could be suddenly transformed into a very ugly creature tomorrow, but it is still "I." Then, say, I get plastic surgery and I become beautiful again. Does the "I" really become beautiful? You need to give a lot of time to reflect on these things. I've thrown them at you in rapid succession, but if you would take the time to understand what I have been saying, to dwell on it, you'll have a gold mine there. I know, because when I stumbled upon these things for the first time, what a treasure I discovered.

Pleasant experiences make life delightful. Painful experiences lead to growth. Pleasant experiences make life delightful, but they don't lead to growth in themselves. What leads to growth is painful experiences. Suffering points up an area in you where you have not yet grown, where you need to grow and be transformed and change. If you knew how to use that suffering, oh, how you would grow. Let's limit ourselves, for the time being, to psychological suffering, to all those negative emotions we have. Don't waste your time on a single one of them. I've already told you what you could do with those emotions. The disappointment you experience when things don't turn out as you wanted them to, watch that! Look at what it says about you. I say this without condemnation (otherwise you're going to get caught up in self-hatred). Observe it as you would observe it in another person. *Look* at that disappointment, that depression you experience when you are criticized. What does that say about you?

Have you heard about the fellow who said, "Who says that worry doesn't help? It certainly does help. Every time I worry about something it doesn't happen!" Well, it certainly helped *him.* Or the other fellow who says, "The neurotic is a person who worries about something that did not happen in the past. He's not like us normal people who worry about things that will not happen in the future." That's the issue. That worry, that anxiety, what does it say about you?

Negative feelings, every negative feeling is useful for awareness, for understanding. They give you the opportunity to feel it, to watch it from the outside. In the beginning, the depression will still be there, but you will have cut your connection with it. Gradually you will understand the depression. As you understand it, it will occur less frequently, and will disappear altogether. Maybe, but by that time it won't matter too much. Before enlightenment I used to be depressed. After enlightenment I continue to be depressed. But gradually, or rapidly, or suddenly, you get the state of wakefulness. This is the state where you drop desires. But remember what I meant by desire and cravings. I meant: "Unless I get what I desire, I refuse to be happy." I mean cases where happiness depends on the fulfillment of desire.

❧

DESIRE, NOT PREFERENCE

Do not suppress desire, because then you would become lifeless. You'd be without energy and that would be terrible. Desire in the healthy sense of the word *is* energy, and the more energy we have, the better. But don't suppress desire, understand it. Understand it. Don't seek to fulfill desire so much as to understand desire. And don't just renounce the objects of your desire, understand them; see them in their true light. See them for what they are really worth. Because if you just suppress your desire, and you attempt to renounce the object of your desire, you are likely to be tied to it. Whereas if you look at it and see it for what it is really worth, if you understand how you are preparing the grounds for misery and disappointment and depression, your desire will then be transformed into what I call a preference.

When you go through life with preferences but don't let your happiness depend on any one of them, then you're awake. You're moving toward wakefulness. Wakefulness, happiness—call it what you wish—is the state of nondelusion, where you see things not as *you* are but as *they* are, insofar as this is possible for a human being. To drop illusions, to see things, to see reality. Every time you are unhappy, you have added something to reality. It is that addition that makes you unhappy. I repeat: You have added something . . . a negative reaction in you. Reality provides the stimulus, you provide the reaction. You have added something by your reaction. And if you examine what you have added, there is always an illusion there, there's a demand, an expectation, a craving. Always. Examples of illusions abound. But as you begin to move ahead on this path, you'll discover them for yourself.

For instance, the illusion, the error of thinking that, by changing the exterior world, *you* will change. You do not change if you merely change your exterior world. If you get yourself a new job or a new spouse or a new home or a new guru or a new spirituality, that does not change *you*. It's like imagining that you change your handwriting by changing your pen. Or that you change your capacity to think by changing your hat. That doesn't change you really, but most people spend all their energies trying to rearrange their exterior world to suit their tastes. Sometimes they succeed—for about five minutes—and they get a little respite, but they are tense even during that respite, because life is always flowing, life is always changing.

So if you want to live, you must have no permanent abode. You must have no place to rest your head. You have to flow with it. As the great Confucius said, "The one who would be constant in happiness must frequently change." Flow. But we keep looking back, don't we? We cling to things in the past and cling to things in the present. "When you set your hand to the plow, you cannot look back." Do you want to enjoy a melody? Do you want to enjoy a symphony? Don't hold on to a few bars of the music. Don't hold on to a couple of notes. Let them pass, let them flow. The whole enjoyment of a symphony lies in your readiness to allow the notes to pass. Whereas if a particular bar took your fancy and you shouted to the orchestra, "Keep playing it again and again and again," that wouldn't be a symphony anymore. Are you familiar with those tales of Nasr-ed-Din, the old mullah? He's a legendary figure whom the Greeks, Turks, and Persians all claim for themselves. He would give his mystical teachings in the form of stories, generally funny stories. And the butt of the story was always old Nasr-ed-Din himself.

One day Nasr-ed-Din was strumming a guitar, playing just one note. After a while a crowd collected around him (this was in a marketplace) and one of the men sitting on the ground there said, "That's a nice note you're playing, Mullah, but why don't you vary it a bit the way other musicians do?" "Those fools," Nasr-ed-Din said, "they're *searching* for the right note. I've *found* it.

CLINGING TO ILLUSION

When you cling, life is destroyed; when you hold on to anything, you cease to live. It's all over the gospel pages. And one attains this by understanding. Understand. Understand another illusion, too, that happiness is not the same as excitement, it's not the same as thrills. That's another illusion, that a thrill comes from living a desire fulfilled. Desire breeds anxiety and sooner or later it brings its hangover. When you've suffered sufficiently, then you are ready to see it. You're feeding yourself with thrills. This is like feeding a racehorse with delicacies. You're giving it cakes and wine. You don't feed a racehorse like that. It's like feeding human beings with drugs. You don't fill your stomach with drugs. You need good, solid, nutritious food and drink. You need to understand all this for yourself.

Another illusion is that someone else can do this for you,

that some savior or guru or teacher can do this for you. Not even the greatest guru in the world can take a single step for you. You've got to take it yourself. St. Augustine said it so marvelously: "Jesus Christ himself could do nothing for many of his hearers." Or to repeat that lovely Arab saying: "The nature of the rain is the same and yet it produces thorns in the marsh and flowers in the garden." It is *you* who have to do it. No one else can help you. It is *you* who have to digest your food, it is *you* who have to understand. No one else can understand for you. It is *you* who have to seek. Nobody can seek for you. And if what you seek is truth, then *you* must do this. You can lean on no one.

There is yet another illusion, that is it important to be respectable, to be loved and appreciated, to be important. Many say we have a natural urge to be loved and appreciated, to belong. That's false. Drop this illusion and you will find happiness. We have a natural urge to be free, a natural urge to love, but not *to be loved*. Sometimes in my psychotherapy sessions I encounter a very common problem: Nobody loves me; how, then, can I be happy? I explain to him or her: "You mean you never have any moments when you forget you're not loved and you let go and are happy?" Of course they have.

A woman, for example, is absorbed in a movie. It's a comedy and she's roaring with laughter and in that blessed moment she's forgotten to remind herself that nobody loves her, nobody loves her, nobody loves her. She's happy! Then she comes out of the theater and her friend whom she saw the movie with goes off with a boyfriend, leaving the woman all alone. So she starts thinking, "All my friends have boyfriends and I have no one. I'm so unhappy. *Nobody loves me!"*

In India, many of our poor people are starting to get transistor radios, which are quite a luxury. "Everybody has a transistor," you hear, "but I don't have a transistor; I'm so unhappy." Until everyone started getting transistors, they were perfectly happy without one. That's the way it is with you. Until somebody told you you wouldn't be happy unless you were loved, you were perfectly happy. You can become happy not being loved, not being desired by or attractive to someone. You become happy by contact with reality. That's what brings happiness, a moment-by-moment contact with reality. That's where you'll find God; that's where you'll find happiness. But most people are not ready to hear that.

Another illusion is that external events have the power to hurt you, that other people have the power to hurt you. They don't. It's you who give this power to them.

Another illusion: You *are* all those labels that people have put on you, or that you have put on yourself. You're not, you're not! So you don't have to cling to them. The day that somebody tells me I'm a genius and I take that seriously, I'm in big trouble. Can you understand why? Because now I'm going to start getting tense. I've got to live up to it, I've got to maintain it. I've got to find out after every lecture: "Did you like the lecture? Do you still think I'm a genius?" See? So what you need to do is smash the label! Smash it, and you're free! Don't identify with those labels. That's what someone else thinks. That's how *he* experienced you at that moment. Are you in fact a genius? Are you a nut? Are you a mystic? Are you crazy? What does it really matter? Provided you continue to be aware, to live life from moment to moment. How marvelously it is described in those words of the gospel: "Look at the birds of the air: they neither sow nor reap nor gather into barns . . . Consider the lilies of the field . . . they neither toil nor spin." That's the real mystic speaking, the awakened person.

So why are you anxious? Can you, for all your anxieties, add a single moment to your life? Why bother about tomorrow? Is there a life after death? Will I survive after death? Why bother about tomorrow? *Get into today.* Someone said, "Life is something that happens to us while we're busy making other plans." That's pathetic. Live in the present moment. This is one of the things you will notice happening to you as you come awake. You find yourself living in the present, tasting every moment as you live it. Another fairly good sign is when you hear the symphony one note after the other without wanting to stop it.

❦
HUGGING MEMORIES

That brings me to another theme, another topic. But this new topic ties in very much with what I've been saying and with my suggestion of becoming aware of all the things we add to reality. Let's take this one step at a time.

A Jesuit was telling me the other day how years ago he gave a talk in New York, where Puerto Ricans were very unpopular at the time because of some incident. Everybody was saying all kinds of things against them. So in his talk he said, "Let me read to you some of the things that the people in New York were saying about certain immigrants." What he read to them was actually what people had said about the Irish, and about the Germans, and about every other wave of immigrants that had come to New York years before! He put it very well when he said, "These people don't bring delinquency with them; they become delinquent when they're faced with certain situations here. We've got to understand them. If you want to cure the situation, it's useless reacting from prejudice. You need understanding, not condemnation." That is how you bring about change in yourself. Not by condemnation, not by calling yourself names, but by understanding what's going on. Not by calling yourself a dirty old sinner. No, no, no, no!

In order to get awareness, you've got to see, and you can't see if you're prejudiced. Almost everything and every person we look at, we look at in a prejudiced way. It's almost enough to dishearten anybody.

Like meeting a long-lost friend. "Hey, Tom," I say, "It's good to see you," and I give him a big hug. Whom am I hugging, Tom or my memory of him? A living human being or a corpse? I'm assuming that he's still the attractive guy I thought he was. I'm assuming he still fits in with the idea I have of him and with my memories and associations. So I give him a hug. Five minutes later I find that he's changed and I have no more interest in him. I hugged the wrong person.

If you want to see how true this is, listen: A religious sister from India goes out to make a retreat. Everybody in the community is saying, "Oh, we know, that's part of her charism; she's always attending workshops and going to retreats; nothing will ever change her." Now, it so happens that the sister does change at this particular workshop, or therapy group, or whatever it is. She changes; everyone notices the difference. Everyone says, "My, you've really come to some insights, haven't you?" She has, and they can see the difference in her behavior, in her body, in her face. You always do when there's an inner change. It always registers in your face, in your eyes, in your body. Well, the sister goes back to her community, and since the community has a prejudiced, fixed idea about her, they're going to continue to look at her through the eyes of that prejudice. They're the only ones who don't see any change in her. They say, "Oh well, she seems a little more spirited, but just wait, she'll be depressed again." And within a few weeks she *is* depressed again; she's reacting to their reaction. And they all say, "See, we told you so; she hadn't changed." But the tragedy is that she had, only they didn't see it. Perception has devastating consequences in the matter of love and human relationships.

Whatever a relationship may be, it certainly entails two things: clarity of perception (inasmuch as we're capable of it; some people would dispute to what extent we can attain clarity of perception, but I don't think anyone would dispute that it is desirable that we move toward it) and accuracy of response. You're more likely to respond accurately when you perceive clearly. When your perception is distorted, you're not likely to respond accurately. How can you love someone whom you do not even see? Do you really see someone you're attached to? Do you really see someone you're afraid of and therefore dislike? We always hate what we fear.

"The fear of the Lord is the beginning of wisdom," people say to me sometimes. But wait a minute. I hope they understand what they're saying, because we always hate what we fear. We always want to destroy and get rid of and avoid what we fear. When you fear somebody, you dislike that person. You dislike that person insofar as you fear that person. And you don't *see* that person either, because your emotion gets in the way. Now, that's just as true when you are attracted to someone. When true love enters, you no longer like or even dislike people in the ordinary sense of the word. You see them clearly and you respond accurately. But at this human level, your likes and dislikes and preferences and attractions, etc., continue to get in the way. So you have to be aware of your prejudices, your likes, your dislikes, your attractions. They're all there, they come from your conditioning. How come you like things that I don't like? Because your culture is different from mine. Your upbringing is different from mine. If I gave you some of the things to eat that I relish, you'd turn away in disgust.

There are people in certain parts of India who love dog flesh. Yet others, if they were told they were being served dog steak, would feel sick. Why? Different conditioning, different programming. Hindus would feel sick if they knew they had eaten beef, but Americans enjoy it. You ask, "But why won't they eat beef?" For the same reason you won't eat your pet dog. The same reason. The cow, to the Indian peasant, is what your pet dog is to you. He doesn't want to eat it. There is a built-in cultural prejudice against it which saves an animal that's needed so much for farming, etc.

So why do I fall in love with a person really? Why is it that I fall in love with one kind of person and not another? Because I'm conditioned. I've got an image, subconsciously, that this particular type of person appeals to me, attracts me. So when I meet this person, I fall head over heels in love. But have I seen her? No! I'll see her after I marry her; that's when the awakening comes! And that's when love may begin. But falling in love has nothing to do with love at all. It isn't love, it's desire, burning desire. You want, with all your heart, to be told by this adorable creature that you're attractive to her. That gives you a tremendous sensation. Meanwhile, everybody else is saying, "What the hell does he see in her?" But it's his conditioning—he's not *seeing*. They say that love is blind. Believe me, there's nothing so clear-sighted as true love, nothing. It's the most clear-sighted thing in the world. Addiction is blind, attachments are blind. Clinging, craving, and desire are blind. But not true love. Don't call them love. But, of course, the word has been desecrated in most modern languages. People talk about making love and falling in love. Like the little boy who says to the little girl, "Have you ever fallen in love?" And she answers, "No, but I've fallen in *like.*"

So what are people talking about when they fall in love? The first thing we need is clarity of perception. One reason we don't perceive people clearly is evident—our emotions get in the way, our conditioning, our likes and dislikes. We've got to grapple with that fact. But we've got to grapple with something much more fundamental—with our ideas, with our conclusions, with our concepts. Believe it or not, every concept that was meant to help us get in touch with reality ends up by being a barrier to getting in touch with reality, because sooner or later we forget that the words are not the thing. The concept is not the same as the reality. They're different. That's why I said to you earlier that the final barrier to finding God is the word "God" itself and the concept of God. It gets in the way if you're not careful. It was meant to be a help; it can be a help, but it can also be a barrier.

GETTING CONCRETE

Every time I have a concept, it is something that I could apply to a number of individuals. We're not talking about a concrete, particular name like Mary or John, which doesn't have a conceptual meaning. A concept applies to any number of individuals, countless individuals. Concepts are universal. For instance, the word "leaf" could be applied to every single leaf on a tree; the same word applies to all those individual leaves. Moreover, the same word applies to all the leaves on all trees, big ones, small ones, tender ones, dried ones, yellow ones, green ones, banana leaves. So if I say to you that I saw a leaf this morning, you really don't have an idea of what I saw.

Let's see if you can understand that. You *do* have an idea of what I did *not* see. I did not see an animal. I did not see a dog. I did not see a human being. I did not see a shoe. So you have some kind of a vague idea of what I saw, but it isn't particularized, it isn't concrete. "Human being" refers not to primitive man, not to civilized man, not to grown-up man, not to a child, not to a male or a female, not to this particular age or another, not to this culture or the other, but to the concept. The human being is found concrete; you never find a universal human being like your concept. So your concept points, but it is never entirely accurate; it misses uniqueness, concreteness. The concept is universal.

When I give you a concept, I give you *something,* and yet how little I have given you. The concept is so valuable, so useful for science. For instance, if I say that everyone here is an animal, that would be perfectly accurate from a scientific viewpoint. But we're something more than animals. If I say that Mary Jane is an animal, that's true; but because I've omitted something essential about her, it's false; it does her an injustice. When I call a person a woman, that's true; but there are lots of things in that person that don't fit into the concept "woman." She is always this particular, concrete, unique woman, who can only be experienced, not conceptualized. The concrete person I've got to see for myself, to experience for myself, to intuit for myself. The individual can be intuited but cannot be conceptualized.

A person is beyond the thinking mind. Many of you would probably be proud to be called Americans, as many Indians would probably be proud to be called Indians. But what is "American," what is "Indian"? It's a convention; it's not part of your nature. All you've got is a label. You really don't know the person. The concept always misses or omits something extremely important, something precious that is only found in reality, which is concrete uniqueness. The great Krishnamurti put it so well when he said, "The day you teach the child the name of the bird, the child will never see that bird again." How true! The first time the child sees that fluffy, alive, moving object, and you say to him, "Sparrow," then tomorrow when the child sees another fluffy, moving object similar to it he says, "Oh, sparrows. I've seen sparrows. I'm *bored* by sparrows."

If you don't look at things through your concepts, you'll never be bored. Every single thing is unique. Every sparrow is unlike every other sparrow despite the similarities. It's a great help to have similarities, so we can abstract, so that we can have a concept. It's a great help, from the point of view of communication, education, science. But it's also very misleading and a great hindrance to seeing *this* concrete individual. If all you experience is your concept, you're not experiencing reality, because reality is concrete. The concept is a help, to *lead* you to reality, but when you get there, you've got to intuit or experience it directly.

A second quality of a concept is that it is static whereas reality is in flux. We use the same name for Niagara Falls, but that body of water is constantly changing. You've got the word "river," but the water there is constantly flowing. You've got one word for your "body," but the cells in your body are constantly being renewed. Let's suppose, for example, there is an enormous wind outside and I want the people in my country to get an idea of what an American gale or hurricane is like. So I capture it in a cigar box and I go back home and say, "Look at this." Naturally, it isn't a gale anymore, is it? Once it's *captured*. Or if I want you to get the feel of what the flow of a river is like and I bring it to you in a bucket. The moment I put it into a bucket it has stopped flowing. The moment you put things into a concept, they stop flowing; they become static, dead. A frozen wave is not a wave. A wave is essentially movement, action; when you freeze it, it is not a wave. Concepts are always frozen. Reality flows. Finally, if we are to believe the mystics (and it doesn't take too much of an effort to understand this, or even believe it, but no one can see it at once), reality is *whole,* but words and concepts *fragment* reality. That is why it is so difficult to translate from one language to another, because each language cuts reality up differently. The English word "home" is impossible to translate into French or Spanish. *"Casa"* is not quite "home"; "home" has associations that are peculiar to the English language. Every language has untranslatable words and expressions, because we're cutting reality up and adding something or subtracting something and usage keeps changing. Reality is a whole and we cut it up to make concepts and we use words to indicate different parts. If you had never seen an animal in your life, for example, and one day you found a tail— just a tail—and somebody told you, "That's a tail," would you have any idea of what it was if you had no idea what an animal was?

Ideas actually fragment the vision, intuition, or experience of reality as a whole. This is what the mystics are perpetually telling us. Words cannot give you reality. They only point, they only indicate. You use them as pointers to get to reality. But once you get there, your concepts are useless. A Hindu priest once had a dispute with a philosopher who claimed that the final barrier to God was the word "God," the concept of God. The priest was quite shocked by this, but the philosopher said, "The ass that you mount and that you use to travel to a house is not the means by which you enter the house. You use the concept to get there; then you dismount, you go beyond it." You don't need to be a mystic to understand that reality is something that cannot be captured by words or concepts. To know reality you have to *know beyond knowing*.

Do those words ring a bell? Those of you who are familiar with *The Cloud of Unknowing* would recognize the expression. Poets, painters, mystics, and the great philosophers all have intimations of its truth. Let's suppose that one day I'm watching a tree. Until now, every time I saw a tree, I said, "Well, it's a tree," But today when I'm looking at the tree, I don't see a tree. At least I don't see what I'm accustomed to seeing. I see something with the freshness of a child's vision. I have no word for it. I see something unique, whole, flowing, not fragmented. And I'm in awe. If you were to ask me, "What did you see?" what do you think I'd answer? I have no word for it. There is no word for reality. Because as soon as I put a word to it, we're back into concepts again.

And if I cannot express this reality that is visible to my senses, how does one express what cannot be seen by the eye or heard by the ear? How does one find a word for the reality of God? Are you beginning to understand what Thomas Aquinas, Augustine, and all the rest were saying and what the Church teaches constantly when she says that God is mystery, is unintelligible to the human mind?

The great Karl Rahner, in one of his last letters, wrote to a young German drug addict who had asked him for help. The addict had said, "You theologians talk about God, but how could this God be relevant in my life? How could this God get me off drugs? Rahner said to him, "I must confess to you in all honesty that for me God is and has always been absolute mystery. I do not understand what God is; no one can. We have intimations, inklings; we make faltering, inadequate attempts to put mystery into words. But there is no word for it, no sentence for it." And talking to a group of theologians in London, Rahner said, "The task of the theologian is to explain everything through God, and to explain God as unexplainable." Unexplainable mystery. One does not know, one cannot say. One says, "Ah, ah . . ."

Words are pointers, they're not descriptions. Tragically,

people fall into idolatry because they think that where God is concerned, the word is the thing. How could you get so crazy? Can you be crazier than that? Even where human beings are concerned, or trees and leaves and animals, the word is not the thing. And you would say that, where God is concerned, the word is one thing? What are you talking about? An internationally famous scripture scholar attended this course in San Francisco, and he said to me, "My God, after listening to you, I understand that I've been an idol worshipper all my life!" He said this openly. "It never struck me that I had been an idol worshipper. My idol was not made of wood or metal; it was a mental idol." These are the more dangerous idol worshippers. They use a very subtle substance, the mind, to produce their God.

What I'm leading you to is the following: awareness of reality around you. Awareness means to watch, to observe what is going on within you and around you. "Going on" is pretty accurate: Trees, grass, flowers, animals, rock, *all* of reality is moving. One observes it, one watches it. How essential it is for the human being not just to observe himself or herself, but to watch all of reality. Are you imprisoned by your concepts? Do you want to break out of your prison? Then *look;* observe; spend hours observing. Watching what? *Anything.* The faces of people, the shapes of trees, a bird in flight, a pile of stones, watch the grass grow. Get in touch with things, look at them. Hopefully you will then break out of these rigid patterns we have all developed, out of what our thoughts and our words have imposed on us. Hopefully we will see. What will we see? This thing that we choose to call reality, whatever is beyond words and concepts. This is a *spiritual* exercise—connected with spirituality—connected with breaking out of your cage, out of the imprisonment of the concepts and words.

How sad if we pass through life and never see it with the eyes of a child. This doesn't mean you should drop your concepts totally; they're very precious. Though we begin without them, concepts have a very positive function. Thanks to them we develop our intelligence. We're invited, not to become children, but to become *like* children. We do have to fall from a stage of innocence and be thrown out of paradise; we do have to develop an "I" and a "me" through these concepts. But then we need to return to paradise. We need to be redeemed again. We need to put off the old man, the old nature, the conditioned self, and return to the state of the child but without *being* a child. When we start off in life, we look at reality with wonder, but it isn't the intelligent wonder of the mystics; it's the formless wonder of the child. Then wonder dies and is replaced by boredom, as we develop language and words and concepts. Then hopefully, if we're lucky, we'll return to wonder again.

❧

AT A LOSS FOR WORDS

Dag Hammarskjöld, the former UN Secretary-General, put it so beautifully: "God does not die on the day we cease to believe in a personal deity. But we die on the day when our lives cease to be illumined by the steady radiance of wonder renewed daily, the source of which is beyond all reason." We don't have to quarrel about a word, because "God" is only a word, a concept. One never quarrels about reality; we only quarrel about opinions, about concepts, about judgments. Drop your concepts, drop your opinions, drop your prejudices, drop your judgments, and you will see that.

"Quia de deo scire non possumus quid sit, sed quid non sit, non possumus considerare de deo, quomodo sit sed quomodo non sit." This is St. Thomas Aquinas' introduction to his whole *Summa Theologica:* "Since we cannot know what God is, but only what God is not, we cannot consider how God is but only how He is not." I have already mentioned Thomas' commentary on Boethius' *De Sancta Trinitate,* where he says that the loftiest degree of the knowledge of God is to know God as the unknown, *tamquam ignotum.* And in his *Questio Disputata de Potentia Dei,* Thomas says, "This is what is ultimate in the human knowledge of God —to know that we do not know God." This gentleman was considered the prince of theologians. He was a mystic, and is a canonized saint today. We're standing on pretty good ground.

In India, we have a Sanskrit saying for this kind of thing: *"neti, neti."* It means: "not that, not that." Thomas' own method was referred to as the *via negativa,* the negative way. C. S. Lewis wrote a diary while his wife was dying. It's called *A Grief Observed.* He had married an American woman whom he loved dearly. He told his friends, "God

gave me in my sixties what He denied me in my twenties."
He hardly had married her when she died a painful death of
cancer. Lewis said that his whole faith crumbled, like a
house of cards. Here he was the great Christian apologist,
but when disaster struck home, he asked himself, "Is God a
loving Father or is God the great vivisectionist?" There's
pretty good evidence for both! I remember that when my
own mother got cancer, my sister said to me, "Tony, why
did God allow this to happen to Mother?" I said to her,
"My dear, last year a million people died of starvation in
China because of the drought, and you never raised a question." Sometimes the best thing that can happen to us is to
be awakened to reality, for calamity to strike, for then we
come to faith, as C. S. Lewis did. He said that he never had
any doubts before about people surviving death, but when
his wife died, he was no longer certain. Why? Because it
was so important to him that she be living. Lewis, as you
know, is the master of comparisons and analogies. He says,
"It's like a rope. Someone says to you, 'Would this bear the
weight of a hundred twenty pounds?' You answer, 'Yes.'
'Well, we're going to let down your best friend on this
rope.' Then you say, 'Wait a minute, let me test that rope
again.' You're not so sure now." Lewis also said in his diary
that we cannot know anything about God and even our
questions about God are absurd. Why? It's as though a
person born blind asks you, "The color green, is it hot or
cold?" *Neti, neti,* not that. "Is it long or is it short?" Not
that. "Is it sweet or is it sour?" Not that. "Is it round or
oval or square?" Not that, not that. The blind person has no

words, no concepts, for a color of which he has no idea, no intuition, no experience. You can only speak to him in analogies. No matter what he asks, you can only say, "Not that." C. S. Lewis says somewhere that it's like asking how many minutes are in the color yellow. Everybody could be taking the question very seriously, discussing it, fighting about it. One person suggests there are twenty-five carrots in the color yellow, the other person says, "No, seventeen potatoes," and they're suddenly fighting. Not that, not that!

This is what is ultimate in our human knowledge of God, to know that we do not know. Our great tragedy is that we know too much. We *think* we know, that is our tragedy; so we never discover. In fact, Thomas Aquinas (he's not only a theologian but also a great philosopher) says repeatedly, "All the efforts of the human mind cannot exhaust the essence of a single fly."

CULTURAL CONDITIONING

Something more about words. I said to you earlier that words are limited. There is more I have to add. There are some words that correspond to *nothing*. For instance, I'm an Indian. Now, let's suppose that I'm a prisoner of war in Pakistan, and they say to me, "Well, today we're going to take you to the frontier, and you're going to take a look at your country." So they bring me to the frontier, and I look across the border, and I think, "Oh, my country, my beauti-

ful country. I see villages and trees and hills. This is my
own, my native land!" After a while one of the guards says,
"Excuse me, we've made a mistake here. We have to move
up another ten miles." What was I reacting to? Nothing. I
kept focusing on a word, India. But trees are not India; trees
are trees. In fact, there are no frontiers or boundaries. They
were put there by the human mind; generally by stupid,
avaricious politicians. My country was one country once
upon a time; it's four now. If we don't watch out it might
be six. Then we'll have six flags, six armies. That's why
you'll never catch me saluting a flag. I abhor all national
flags because they are idols. What are we saluting? I salute
humanity, not a flag with an army around it.

Flags are in the heads of people. In any case, there are
thousands of words in our vocabulary that do not correspond to reality at all. But do they trigger emotions in us!
So we begin to see things that are not there. We actually *see*
Indian mountains when they don't exist, and we actually see
Indian people who also don't exist. Your American conditioning exists. My Indian conditioning exists. But that's not
a very happy thing. Nowadays, in Third World countries,
we talk a great deal about "inculturation." What is this
thing called "culture"? I'm not very happy with the word.
Does it mean you'd like to do something because you were
conditioned to do it? That you'd like to feel something
because you were conditioned to feel it? Isn't that being
mechanical? Imagine an American baby that is adopted by a
Russian couple and taken to Russia. It has no notion that it
was born American. It's brought up talking Russian; it lives

and dies for Mother Russia; it hates Americans. The child is stamped with his own culture; it's steeped in its own literature. It looks at the world through the eyes of its culture. Now, if you want to wear your culture the way you wear your clothes, that's fine. The Indian woman would wear a sari and the American woman would wear something else, the Japanese woman would wear her kimono. But nobody identifies herself with the clothes. But you do want to wear your culture more intently. You become proud of your culture. They teach you to be proud of it. Let me put this as forcefully as possible. There's this Jesuit friend of mine who said to me, "Anytime I see a beggar or a poor person, I cannot not give this person alms. I got that from my mother." His mother would offer a meal to any poor person who passed by. I said to him, "Joe, what you have is not a virtue; what you have is a compulsion, a *good* one from the point of view of the beggar, but a compulsion nonetheless." I remember another Jesuit who said to us once at an intimate gathering of the men of our Jesuit province in Bombay, "I'm eighty years old; I've been a Jesuit for sixty-five years. I have never once missed my hour of meditation— never once." Now, that *could* be very admirable, or it could also be a compulsion. No great merit in it if it's mechanical. The beauty of an action comes not from its having become a habit but from its sensitivity, consciousness, clarity of perception, and accuracy of response. I can say yes to one beggar and no to another. I am not compelled by any conditioning or programming from my past experiences or from my culture. Nobody has stamped anything on me, or if they have, I'm no longer reacting on the basis of that. If you had a bad experience with an American or were bitten by a dog or had a bad experience with a certain type of food, for the rest of your life you'd be influenced by that experience. And that's bad! You need to be liberated from that. Don't carry over experiences from the past. In fact, don't carry over good experiences from the past either. Learn what it means to experience something fully, then drop it and move on to the next moment, uninfluenced by the previous one. You'd be traveling with such little baggage that you could pass through the eye of a needle. You'd know what eternal life is, because eternal life is *now,* in the timeless *now.* Only thus will you enter into eternal life. But how many things we carry along with us. We never set about the task of freeing ourselves, of dropping the baggage, of being ourselves. I'm sorry to say that everywhere I go I find Muslims who use their religion, their worship, and their Koran to distract themselves from this task. And the same applies to Hindus and Christians.

Can you imagine the human being who is no longer influenced by words? You can give him any number of words and he'll still give you a fair deal. You can say, "I'm Cardinal Archbishop So-and-so," but he'll still give you a fair deal; he'll see you as you are. He's uninfluenced by the label.

FILTERED REALITY

I want to say one more thing about our perception of reality. Let me put it in the form of an analogy. The President of the United States has to get feedback from the citizens. The Pope in Rome has to get feedback from the whole Church. There are literally millions of items that could be fed to them, but they could hardly take all of them in, much less digest them. So they have people whom they trust to make abstracts, summarize things, monitor, filter; in the end, some of it gets to their desk. Now, this is what's happening to us. From every pore or living cell of our bodies and from all our senses we are getting feedback from reality. But we are filtering things out constantly. Who's doing the filtering? Our conditioning? Our culture? Our programming? The way we were taught to see things and to experience them? Even our language can be a filter. There is so much filtering going on that sometimes you won't see things that are there. You only have to look at a paranoid person who's always feeling threatened by something that isn't there, who's constantly interpreting reality in terms of certain experiences of the past or certain conditioning that he or she has had.

But there's another demon, too, who's doing the filtering. It's called attachment, desire, craving. The root of sorrow is craving. Craving distorts and destroys perception. Fears and desires haunt us. Samuel Johnson said, "The knowledge that he is to swing from a scaffold within a week wonderfully concentrates a man's mind." You blot out everything else and concentrate only on the fear, or desire, or craving. In many ways we were drugged when we were young. We were brought up to need people. For what? For acceptance, approval, appreciation, applause—for what they called success. Those are words that do not correspond to reality. They are conventions, things that are invented, but we don't realize that they don't correspond to reality. What is success? It is what one group decided is a good thing. Another group will decide the same thing is bad. What is good in Washington might be considered bad in a Carthusian monastery. Success in a political circle might be considered failure in some other circles. These are conventions. But we treat them like realities, don't we? When we were young, we were programmed to unhappiness. They taught us that in order to be happy you need money, success, a beautiful or handsome partner in life, a good job, friendship, spirituality, God—you name it. Unless you get these things, you're not going to be happy, we were told. Now, that is what I call an attachment. An attachment is a belief that without something you are not going to be happy. Once you get convinced of that—and it gets into our subconscious, it gets stamped into the roots of our being—you are finished. "How could I be happy unless I have good health?" you say. But I'll tell you something. I have met people dying of cancer who were happy. But how could they be happy if they knew they were going to die? But they were. "How could I be happy if I don't have money?" One person has a million dollars in the bank, and he feels insecure; the other person has practically no money, but he doesn't seem to feel any insecurity at all. He was

programmed differently, that's all. Useless to exhort the first
person about what to do; he needs understanding. Exhortations are of no great help. You need to understand that
you've been programmed; it's a false belief. See it as false,
see it as a fantasy. What are people doing all through their
lives? They're busy fighting; fight, fight, fight. That's what
they call survival. When the average American says he or
she is making a living, it isn't a living they're making, oh
no! They have much more than they need to live. Come to
my country and you'll see that. You don't need all those cars
to live. You don't need a television set to live. You don't
need makeup to live. You don't need all those clothes to
live. But try to convince the average American of this.
They've been brainwashed; they've been programmed. So
they work and strive to get the desired object that will
make them happy. Listen to this pathetic story—your story,
my story, everybody's story: "Until I get this object
(money, friendship, anything) I'm not going to be happy;
I've got to strive to get it and then when I've got it, I've got
to strive to keep it. I get a temporary thrill. Oh, I'm so
thrilled, I've got it!" But how long does that last? A few
minutes, a few days at the most. When you get your brand-
new car, how long does the thrill last? Until your *next*
attachment is threatened!

The truth about a thrill is that I get tired of it after a
while. They told me *prayer* was the big thing; they told me
God was the big thing; they told me *friendship* was the big
thing. And not knowing what prayer really was or not
knowing what God really was, not knowing what friend-

ship really was, we made much out of them. But after a while we got bored with them—bored with prayer, with God, with friendship. Isn't that pathetic? And there's no way out, there's simply no way out. It's the only model we were given—to be happy. We weren't given any other model. Our culture, our society, and, I'm sorry to say, even our religion gave us no other model. You've been appointed a cardinal. What a great honor that is! Honor? Did you say honor? You used the wrong word. Now others are going to aspire to it. You lapsed into what the gospels call "the world" and you're going to lose your soul. The world, power, prestige, winning, success, honor, etc., are nonexistent things. You gain the world but you lose your soul. Your whole life has been empty and soulless. There is nothing there. There's only one way out and that is to get deprogrammed! How do you do that? You become aware of the programming. You cannot change by an effort of the will; you cannot change through ideals; you cannot change through building up new habits. Your behavior may change, but you don't. You only change through awareness and understanding. When you see a stone as a stone and a scrap of paper as a scrap of paper, you don't think that the stone is a precious diamond anymore and you don't think that that scrap of paper is a check for a billion dollars. When you *see* that, you change. There's no violence anymore in your attempt to change yourself. Otherwise, what you call change is simply moving the furniture around. Your behavior is changed, but not *you*.

DETACHMENT

The only way to change is by changing your understanding. But what does it mean to understand? How do we go about it? Consider how we're enslaved by various attachments; we're striving to rearrange the world so that we can keep these attachments, because the world is a constant threat to them. I fear that a friend may stop loving me; he or she may turn to somebody else. I have to keep making myself attractive because I have to get this other person. Somebody brainwashed me into thinking I need his or her love. But I really don't. I don't need anybody's love; I just need to get in touch with reality. I need to break out of this prison of mine, this programming, this conditioning, these false beliefs, these fantasies; I need to break out into reality. Reality is lovely; it is an absolute delight. Eternal life is now. We're surrounded by it, like the fish in the ocean, but we have no notion about it at all. We're too distracted with this attachment. Temporarily, the world rearranges itself to suit our attachment, so we say, "Yeah, great! My team won!" But hang on; it'll change; you'll be depressed tomorrow. Why do we keep doing this?

Do this little exercise for a few minutes: Think of something or someone you are attached to; in other words, something or someone without which or without whom you think you are not going to be happy. It could be your job, your career, your profession, your friend, your money, whatever. And say to this object or person, "I really do not need you to be happy. I'm only deluding myself in the belief that without you I will not be happy. But I really don't need you for my happiness; I can be happy without you. You are not my happiness, you are not my joy." If your attachment is a person, he or she is not going to be very happy to hear you say this, but go ahead anyway. You can say it in the secrecy of your heart. In any case, you'll be making contact with the truth; you'll be smashing through a fantasy. Happiness is a state of nonillusion, of dropping the illusion.

Or you could try another exercise: Think of a time when you were heartbroken and thought you would never be happy again (your husband died, your wife died, your best friend deserted you, you lost your money). What happened? Time went on, and if you managed to pick up another attachment or managed to find somebody else you were attracted to or something else you were attracted to, what happened to the old attachment? You didn't really need it to be happy, did you? That should have taught you, but we never learn. We're programmed; we're conditioned. How liberating it is not to depend emotionally on anything. If you could get one second's experience of that, you'd be breaking through your prison and getting a glimpse of the sky. Someday, maybe, you will even fly.

I was afraid to say this, but I talked to God, and I told Him that I don't need Him. My initial reaction was: "This is so contrary to everything that I've been brought up with." Now, some people want to make an exception of their attachment to God. They say, "If God is the God that I think He ought to be, He's not going to like it when I give up my attachment to Him!" All right, if you think that unless you get God you're not going to be happy, then this "God" you're thinking of has nothing to do with the real God. You're thinking of a dream state; you're thinking of your concept. Sometimes you have to get rid of "God" in order to find God. Lots of mystics tell us that.

We've been so blinded by everything that we have not discovered the basic truth that attachments hurt rather than help relationships. I remember how frightened I was to say to an intimate friend of mine, "I really don't need you. I can be perfectly happy without you. And by telling you this I find I can enjoy your company thoroughly—no more anxieties, no more jealousies, no more possessiveness, no more clinging. It is a delight to be with you when I am enjoying you on a nonclinging basis. You're free; so am I." But to many of you I'm sure this is like talking a foreign language. It took me many, many months to fully understand this, and mind you, I'm a Jesuit, whose spiritual exercises are all about exactly this, although I missed the point because my culture and my society in general had taught me to view people in terms of my attachments. I'm quite amused, sometimes, to see even seemingly objective people like therapists and spiritual directors say of someone, "He's a great guy, great guy, I really like him." I find out later that it's because he likes me that I like him. I look into myself, and I find the same thing coming up now and again: If you're attached to appreciation and praise, you're going to view people in terms of their threat to your attachment or their fostering of your attachment. If you're a politician and you want to be elected, how do you think you're going to look at people, how will your interest in people be guided? You will be concerned for the person who's going to get you the vote. If what you're interested in is sex, how do you think you're going to look at men and women? If you're attached to power, that colors your view of human beings. An attachment destroys your capacity to love. What is love? Love is sensitivity, love is consciousness. To give you an example: I'm listening to a symphony, but if all I hear is the sound of the drums I don't hear the symphony. What is a loving heart? A loving heart is sensitive to the *whole* of life, to *all* persons; a loving heart doesn't harden itself to any person or thing. But the moment you become attached in my sense of the word, then you're blocking out many other things. You've got eyes only for the object of your attachment; you've got ears only for the drums; the heart has hardened. Moreover, it's blinded, because it no longer sees the object of its attachment objectively. Love entails clarity of perception, objectivity; there is nothing so clear-sighted as love.

❦

ADDICTIVE LOVE

The heart in love remains soft and sensitive. But when you're hell-bent on *getting* this or the other thing, you become ruthless, hard, and insensitive. How can you love people when you need people? You can only use them. If I need you to make me happy, I've got to use you, I've got to manipulate you, I've got to find ways and means of winning you. I cannot let you be free. I can only love people when I have emptied my life of people. When I die to the need for people, then I'm right in the desert. In the beginning it feels awful, it feels lonely, but if you can take it for a while, you'll suddenly discover that it isn't lonely at all. It is solitude, it is aloneness, and the desert begins to flower. Then at last you'll know what love is, what God is, what reality is. But in the beginning giving up the drug can be tough, unless you have a very keen understanding or unless you have suffered enough. It's a great thing to have suffered. Only then can you get sick of it. You can make use of suffering to end suffering. Most people simply go on suffering. That explains the conflict I sometimes have between the role of spiritual director and that of therapist. A therapist says, "Let's ease the suffering." The spiritual director says, "Let her suffer, she'll get sick of this way of relating to people and she'll finally decide to break out of this prison of emotional dependence on others." Shall I offer a palliative or remove a cancer? It's not easy to decide.

A person slams a book on the table in disgust. Let him keep slamming it on the table. Don't pick up the book for him and tell him it's all right. Spirituality is awareness, awareness, awareness, awareness, awareness, awareness. When your mother got angry with you, she didn't say there was something wrong with her, she said there was something wrong with *you;* otherwise she wouldn't have been angry. Well, I made the great discovery that if *you* are angry, Mother, there's something wrong with *you.* So you'd better cope with *your* anger. Stay with it and cope with it. It's not mine. Whether there's something wrong with me or not, I'll examine that independently of your anger. I'm not going to be influenced by your anger.

The funny thing is that when I can do this without feeling any negativity toward another, I can be quite objective about myself, too. Only a very aware person can refuse to pick up the guilt and anger, can say, "You're having a tantrum. Too bad. I don't feel the slightest desire to rescue you anymore, and I refuse to feel guilty." I'm not going to hate myself for anything I've done. That's what guilt is. I'm not going to give myself a bad feeling and whip myself for anything I have done, either *right* or *wrong*. I'm ready to analyze it, to watch it, and say, "Well, if I did wrong, it was in unawareness." Nobody does wrong *in awareness*. That's why theologians tell us very beautifully that Jesus could do no wrong. That makes very good sense to me, because the enlightened person can do no wrong. The enlightened person is free. Jesus was free and because he was free, he couldn't do any wrong. But since you *can* do wrong, you're not free.

MORE WORDS

Mark Twain put it very nicely when he said, "It was so cold that if the thermometer had been an inch longer, we would have frozen to death." We do freeze to death on words. It's not the cold outside that matters, but the thermometer. It's not reality that matters, but what you're saying to yourself about it. I was told a lovely story about a farmer in Finland. When they were drawing up the Russian-Finnish border, the farmer had to decide whether he wanted to be in Russia or Finland. After a long time he said he wanted to be in Finland, but he didn't want to offend the Russian officials. These came to him and wanted to know why he wanted to be in Finland. The farmer replied, "It has always been my desire to live in Mother Russia, but at my age I wouldn't be able to survive another Russian winter."

Russia and Finland are only words, concepts, but not for human beings, not for crazy human beings. We're almost never looking at reality. A guru was once attempting to explain to a crowd how human beings react to words, feed on words, live on words, rather than on reality. One of the men stood up and protested; he said, "I don't agree that words have all that much effect on us." The guru said, "Sit down, you son of a bitch." The man went livid with rage and said, "You call yourself an enlightened person, a guru, a master, but you ought to be ashamed of yourself." The guru then said, "Pardon me, sir, I was carried away. I really beg your pardon; that was a lapse; I'm sorry." The man finally calmed down. Then the guru said, "It took just a few words to get a whole tempest going within you; and it took just a few words to calm you down, didn't it?" Words, words, words, words, how imprisoning they are if they're not used properly.

HIDDEN AGENDAS

There is a difference between knowledge and awareness, between information and awareness. I just said to you that one cannot do evil in awareness. But one can do evil in knowledge or information, when you *know* something is bad. "Father, forgive them, for they know not what they do." I would translate that as "They're not *aware* of what they are doing." Paul says he is the greatest of sinners because he persecuted the Church of Christ. But, he adds, I did it unawares. Or if they had been *aware* that they were crucifying the Lord of Glory, they would never have done so. Or: "The time will come when they will persecute you and they *think* they are doing a service to God." They aren't aware. They're caught up in information and knowledge. Thomas Aquinas puts it nicely when he says, "Every time someone sins, they're sinning under the guise of good." They're blinding themselves; they're seeing something as good even though they know it is bad; they're rationalizing because they're seeking something under the pretext of good.

Someone gave me two situations in which she found it difficult to be aware. She was in a service industry where many people were lined up, many phones were ringing, and she was alone and there were distractions coming from a lot of uptight, angry people. She found it extremely difficult to maintain serenity and calm. The other situation was when she was driving in traffic, with horns blowing and people shouting four-letter words. She asked me whether eventually that nervousness would dissipate and she could remain at peace.

Did you pick up the attachment there? Peace. Her attachment to peace and calm. She was saying, "Unless I'm peaceful, I won't be happy." Did it ever occur to you that you could be happy *in tension?* Before enlightenment, I used to be depressed; after enlightenment, I continue to be depressed. You don't make a goal out of relaxation and sensitivity. Have you ever heard of people who get tense trying to relax? If one is tense, one simply observes one's tension. You will never understand yourself if you seek to change yourself. The harder you try to change yourself, the worse it gets. You are called upon to be aware. Get the feel of that jangling telephone; get the feel of jarred nerves; get the sensation of the steering wheel in the car. In other words, come to *reality,* and let tension or the calmness take care of itself. As a matter of fact, you will have to let them take care of themselves because you'll be too preoccupied with getting in touch with reality. Step by step, let whatever happens happen. Real change will come when it is brought about, not by your ego, but by reality. Awareness releases reality to change you.

In awareness you change, but you've got to experience it. At this point you're just taking my word for it. Perhaps also you've got a plan to become aware. Your ego, in its own cunning way, is trying to push you into awareness. Watch it! You'll meet with resistance; there will be trouble. When someone is anxious about being aware all the time, you can spot the mild anxiety. They want to be awake, to find out if they're really awake or not. That's part of *asceticism,* not awareness. It sounds strange in a culture where we've been trained to achieve goals, to get somewhere, but in fact there's nowhere to go because you're there already. The Japanese have a nice way of putting it: "The day you cease to travel, you will have arrived." Your attitude should be: "I want to be aware, I want to be in touch with whatever is and let whatever happens happen; if I'm awake, fine, and if I'm asleep, fine." The moment you make a goal out of it and attempt to *get* it, you're seeking ego glorification, ego promotion. You want the good feeling that you've *made it.* When you do "make it," you won't know. Your left hand won't know what your right hand is doing. "Lord, when did we do this? We had no awareness." Charity is never so lovely as when one has lost consciousness that one is practicing charity. "You mean I helped you? I was enjoying myself. I was just doing my dance. It helped you, that's wonderful. Congratulations to you. No credit to me."

When you attain, when you are aware, increasingly you will not be bothered about labels like "awake" or "asleep." One of my difficulties here is to arouse your curiosity but not your spiritual greed. Let's come awake, it's going to be wonderful. After a while, it doesn't matter; one is aware, because one lives. The unaware life is not worth living. And you will leave pain to take care of itself.

GIVING IN

The harder you try to change, the worse it can get. Does this mean that a certain degree of passivity is all right? Yes, the more you resist something, the greater power you give to it. That's the meaning, I think, of Jesus' words: "When someone strikes you on the right cheek, offer him your left as well." You always empower the demons you fight. That's very Oriental. But if you flow with the enemy, you overcome the enemy. How does one cope with evil? Not by fighting it but by understanding it. In understanding, it disappears. How does one cope with darkness? Not with one's fist. You don't chase darkness out of the room with a broom, you turn on a light. The more you fight darkness, the more real it becomes to you, and the more you exhaust yourself. But when you turn on the light of awareness, it melts. Say this scrap of paper is a billion-dollar check. Ah, I must renounce it, the gospel says, I must give it up if I want eternal life. Are you going to substitute one greed—a spiritual greed—for the other greed? Before, you had a worldly ego and now you've got a spiritual ego, but you've got an ego all the same, a refined one and one more difficult to cope with. When you renounce something, you're tied to it. But if instead of renouncing it, I look at it and say, "Hey, this isn't a billion-dollar check, this is a scrap of paper," there is nothing to fight, nothing to renounce.

ASSORTED LANDMINES

In my country, lots of men grow up with the belief that women are cattle. "I married her," they say. "She's my possession." Are these men to blame? Get ready for a shock: They aren't. Just as many Americans are not to blame for the way they view Russians. Their glasses or perceptions simply have been dyed a certain color, and there they are; that's the color through which they look at the world. What does it take to make them real, to make them aware that they're looking at the world through colored glasses? There is no salvation till they have seen their basic prejudice.

As soon as you look at the world through an ideology you are finished. No reality fits an ideology. Life is beyond that. That is why people are always searching for a meaning to life. But life has no meaning; it cannot have meaning because meaning is a formula; meaning is something that makes sense to the mind. Every time you make sense out of reality, you bump into something that destroys the sense you made. Meaning is only found when you go beyond meaning. Life only makes sense when you perceive it as mystery and it makes no sense to the conceptualizing mind.

I don't say that adoration isn't important, but I do say that doubt is infinitely more important than adoration. Everywhere people are searching for objects to adore, but I don't find people awake enough in their attitudes and convictions. How happy we would be if terrorists would adore their ideology less and question more. However, we don't like to apply that to ourselves; we think we're all right and the terrorists are wrong. But a terrorist to you is a martyr to the other side.

Loneliness is when you're missing people, aloneness is when you're enjoying yourself. Remember that quip of George Bernard Shaw. He was at one of those awful cocktail parties, where nothing gets said. Someone asked him if he was enjoying himself. He answered, "It's the only thing I am enjoying here." You never enjoy others when you are enslaved to them. Community is not formed by a set of slaves, by people demanding that other people make them happy. Community is formed by emperors and princesses. You're an emperor, not a beggar; you're a princess, not a beggar. There's no begging bowl in a true community. There's no clinging, no anxiety, no fear, no hangover, no possessiveness, no demands. Free people form community, not slaves. This is such a simple truth, but it has been drowned out by a whole culture, including religious culture. Religious culture can be very manipulative if you don't watch out.

Some people see awareness as a high point, a plateau, *beyond* experiencing every moment as it is. That's making a goal out of awareness. But with true awareness there's nowhere to go, nothing to achieve. How do we get to this awareness? Through awareness. When people say they really want to experience every moment, they're really talking awareness, except for that "wanting." You don't want to experience awareness; you do or you don't.

A friend of mine has just gone to Ireland. He told me that though he's an American citizen he's entitled to an Irish passport and was getting one because he is scared to travel abroad on an American passport. If terrorists walk in and say, "Let me see your passport," he wants to be able to say, "I'm Irish." But when people sit next to him on the plane, they don't want to see labels; they want to taste and experience *this* person, as he really is. How many people spend their lives not eating food but eating the menu? A menu is only an indication of something that's available. You want to eat the steak, not the words.

❦

THE DEATH OF ME

Can one be fully human without experiencing tragedy? The only tragedy there is in the world is ignorance; all evil comes from that. The only tragedy there is in the world is unwakefulness and unawareness. From them comes fear, and from fear comes everything else, but death is not a tragedy at all. Dying is wonderful; it's only horrible to people who have never understood life. It's only when you're afraid of life that you fear death. It's only dead people who fear death. But people who are alive have no fear of death. One of your American authors put it so well. He said awakening is the death of your belief in injustice and tragedy. The end of the world for a caterpillar is a butterfly for the master. Death is resurrection. We're talking not about some resurrection that will happen but about one that is happening right now. If you would die to the past, if you would die to every minute, you would be the person who is fully alive, because a fully alive person is one who is full of death. We're always dying to things. We're always shedding everything in order to be fully alive and to be resurrected at every moment. The mystics, saints, and others make great efforts to wake people up. If they don't wake up, they're always going to have these other minor ills like hunger, wars, and violence. The greatest evil is sleeping people, ignorant people.

A Jesuit once wrote a note to Father Arrupe, his superior general, asking him about the relative value of communism, socialism, and capitalism. Father Arrupe gave him a lovely reply. He said, "A system is about as good or as bad as the people who use it." People with golden hearts would make capitalism or communism or socialism work beautifully.

Don't ask the world to change—you change first. Then you'll get a good enough look at the world so that you'll be able to change whatever you think ought to be changed. Take the obstruction out of your own eye. If you don't, you have lost the right to change anyone or anything. Till you are aware of yourself, you have no right to interfere with anyone else or with the world. Now, the danger of attempting to change others or change things when you yourself are not aware is that you may be changing things for your own convenience, your pride, your dogmatic convictions and beliefs, or just to relieve your negative feelings. I have negative feelings, so you better change in such a way that I'll feel good. First, cope with your negative feelings so that when you move out to change others, you're not coming from hate or negativity but from love. It may seem strange, too, that people can be very hard on others and still be very loving. The surgeon can be hard on a patient and yet loving. Love can be very hard indeed.

❧

INSIGHT AND UNDERSTANDING

But what does self-change entail? I've said it in so many words, over and over, but now I'm going to break it down into little segments. First, insight. Not effort, not cultivating habits, not having an ideal. Ideals do a lot of damage. The whole time you're focusing on what should be instead of focusing on what is. And so you're imposing what should be on a present reality, never having understood what present reality is. Let me give you an example of insight from my own experience in counseling. A priest comes to me and says he's lazy; he wants to be more industrious, more active, but he is lazy. I ask him what "lazy" means. In the old days I would have said to him, "Let's see, why don't you make a list of things you want to do every day, and then every night you check them off, and it will give you a good feeling; build up habit that way." Or I might say to him, "Who is your ideal, your patron saint?" And if he says St. Francis Xavier, I would tell him, "See how much Xavier worked. You must meditate on him and that will get you moving." That's one way of going about it, but, I'm sorry to say, it's superficial. Making him use his willpower, effort, doesn't last very long. His behavior may change, but he does not. So I now move in the other direction. I say to him, "Lazy, what's that? There are a million types of laziness. Let's hear what your type of laziness is. Describe what *you* mean by lazy?" He says, "Well, I never get anything done. I don't feel like doing anything." I ask, "You mean right from the moment you get up in the morning?" "Yes," he answers. "I wake up in the morning and there's nothing worth getting up for." "You're depressed, then?" I ask. "You could call it that," he says. "I have sort of withdrawn." "Have you always been like this?" I ask. "Well, not always. When I was younger, I was more active. When I was in the seminary, I was full of life." "So when did this begin?" "Oh, about three or four years ago." I ask him if anything happened then. He thinks a while. I say, "If you have to think so much, nothing very special could have happened four years ago. How about the year before that?" He says, "Well, I was ordained that year." "Anything happen in your ordination year?" I ask. "There was one little thing, the final examination in theology; I failed it. It was a bit of a disappointment, but I've gotten over it. The bishop was planning to send me to Rome, to eventually teach in the seminary. I rather liked the idea, but since I failed the examination, he changed his mind and sent me to this parish. Actually, there was some injustice because . . ." Now he's getting worked up; there's anger there that he hasn't gotten over. He's got to work through that disappointment. It's useless to preach him a sermon. It's useless to give him an idea. We've got to get him to face his anger and disappointment and to get some insight into all of that. When he's able to work through that, he's back into life again. If I gave him an exhortation and told him how hard his married brothers and sisters work, that would merely make him feel guilty. He doesn't have the self-insight which is going to heal him. So that's the first thing.

There's another great task, understanding. Did you really think this was going to make you happy? You just assumed it was going to make you happy. Why did you want to teach in the seminary? Because you wanted to be happy. You thought that being a professor, having a certain status and prestige, would make you happy. Would it? Understanding is called for there.

In making the distinction between "I" and "me," it's a great help to disidentify what is going on. Let me give you an example of this kind of thing. A young Jesuit priest comes to see me; he's a lovely, extraordinary, gifted, talented, charming, lovable man—everything. But he had a strange kind of a kink. With employees he was a terror. He was even known to assault them. It nearly became a matter for the police. Whenever he was put in charge of the grounds, the school, or whatever, this problem would keep coming up. He made a thirty-day retreat in what we Jesuits call a Tertianship, where he meditated day after day on the patience and love of Jesus for those who were underprivileged, etc. But I knew it wasn't going to have an effect. Anyway, he went home and was better for about three or four months. (Somebody said about most retreats that we begin them in the name of the Father and of the Son and of the Holy Spirit, and we end as it was in the beginning, is now, and ever shall be, world without end. Amen.) After that, he was right back to square one. So he came to see me. I was very busy at the time. Though he had come from another city in India, I couldn't see him. So I said, "I'm going for my evening walk; if you want to come with me on the walk, that's fine, but I don't have any other time." So we went for a walk. I'd known him before, and as we were walking, I had a strange feeling. When I get one of these strange feelings, I generally check it out with the person in question. So I said, "I have a strange feeling that you're hiding something from me. Are you?" He became indignant. He said, "What do you mean, hiding? Do you think I'd undertake this long journey and come to ask for your time in order to hide something?" I said, "Well, it's a funny feeling I had, that's all; I thought I should check with you." We walked on. We have a lake not far from where I live. I remember the scene distinctly. He said, "Could we sit down somewhere?" I said, "O.K." We sat on a low wall that skirts the lake. He said, "You're right. I am hiding something from you." And with that he burst into tears. He said, "I'm going to tell you something I've never said to anybody since I became a Jesuit. My father died when I was very young, and my mother became a servant. Her job was to clean lavatories and toilets and bathrooms, and sometimes she'd work for sixteen hours a day to get the wherewithal to support us. I'm so ashamed of that that I've hidden it from everybody and I continue taking revenge, irrationally,

on her and the whole servant class." The feeling got trans-
ferred. No one could make sense of why this charming man
was doing this, but the moment he saw that, there was never
any trouble again, never. He was all right.

NOT PUSHING IT

Meditating on and imitating externally the behavior of
Jesus is no help. It's not a question of imitating Christ, it's a
question of becoming what Jesus was. It's a question of
becoming Christ, becoming aware, understanding what's
going on within you. All the other methods we use for self-
change could be compared to pushing a car. Let's suppose
you have to travel to a distant city. The car breaks down
along the way. Well, too bad; the car's broken down. So we
roll up our sleeves and begin to push the car. And we push
and push and push and push, till we get to the distant city.
"Well," we say, "we made it." And then we push the car all
the way to another city! You say, "We got there, didn't
we?" But do you call this life? You know what you need?
You need an expert, you need a mechanic to lift the hood
and change the spark plug. Turn the ignition key and the
car moves. You need the expert—you need understanding,
insight, awareness—you don't need pushing. You don't
need effort. That's why people are so tired, so weary. You
and I were trained to be dissatisfied with ourselves. That's
where the evil comes from psychologically. We're always

dissatisfied, we're always discontented, we're always pushing. Go on, put out more effort, more and more effort. But there's always that conflict inside; there's very little understanding.

🍎
GETTING REAL

One red-letter day in my life occurred in India. It was a great day, really, the day after I was ordained. I sat in a confessional. We had a very saintly Jesuit priest in our parish, a Spaniard, whom I had known even before I went to the Jesuit novitiate. The day before I left for the novitiate, I thought I'd better make a clean breast of everything so that when I got to the novitiate I'd be nice and clean and wouldn't have to tell the novice master anything. This old Spanish priest would have crowds of people lined up at his confessional; he had a violet-colored handkerchief which he covered his eyes with, and he'd mumble something and give you a penance and send you away. He'd only met me a couple of times, but he'd call me Antonie. So I stood in line, and when my turn came, I tried changing my voice as I made my confession. He listened to me patiently, gave me my penance, absolved me, and then said, "Antonie, when are you going to the novitiate?"

Well, anyway, I went to this parish the day after my ordination. And the old priest says to me, "Do you want to hear confessions?" I said, "All right." He said, "Go and sit in my confessional." I thought, "My, I'm a holy man. I'm going to sit in his confessional." I heard confessions for three hours. It was Palm Sunday and we had the Easter crowd coming in. I came out depressed, not from what I had heard, because I had been led to expect that, and, having some inkling of what was going on in my own heart, I was shocked by nothing. You know what depressed me? The realization that I was giving them these little pious platitudes: "Now pray to the Blessed Mother, she loves you," and "Remember that God is on your side." Were these pious platitudes any cure for cancer? And this *is* a cancer I'm dealing with, the lack of awareness and reality. So I swore a mighty oath to myself that day: "I'll learn, I'll learn, so it will not be said of me when it is all over, 'Father, what you said to me was absolutely true but totally useless.' "

Awareness, insight. When you become an expert (and you'll soon become an expert) you don't need to take a course in psychology. As you begin to observe yourself, to watch yourself, to pick up those negative feelings, you'll find your own way of explaining it. And you'll notice the change. But then you'll have to deal with the big villain, and that villain is self-condemnation, self-hatred, self-dissatisfaction.

ASSORTED IMAGES

Let's talk more about effortlessness in change. I thought of a nice image for that, a sailboat. When a sailboat has a mighty wind in its sail, it glides along so effortlessly that the boatman has nothing to do but steer. He makes no effort; he doesn't push the boat. That's an image of what happens when change comes about through awareness, through understanding.

I was going through some of my notes and I found some quotations that go well with what I've been saying. Listen to this one: "There is nothing so cruel as nature. In the whole universe there is no escape from it, and yet it is not nature that does the injury, but the person's own heart." Does that make sense? It isn't nature that does the injury, but the person's own heart. There's the story of Paddy, who fell off the scaffolding and got a good bump. They asked, "Did the fall hurt you, Paddy?" And he said, "No, it was the stop that hurt, not the fall." When you cut water, the water doesn't get hurt; when you cut something solid, it breaks. You've got solid attitudes inside you; you've got solid illusions inside you; that's what bumps against nature, that's where you get hurt, that's where the pain comes from.

Here's a lovely one: It's from an Oriental sage, though I don't remember which one. As with the Bible the author doesn't matter. What is said is what matters. "If the eye is unobstructed, it results in sight; if the ear is unobstructed, the result is hearing; if the nose is unobstructed, the result is a sense of smell; if the mouth is unobstructed, the result is a sense of taste; if the mind is unobstructed, the result is wisdom."

Wisdom occurs when you drop barriers you have erected through your concepts and conditioning. Wisdom is not something acquired; wisdom is not experience; wisdom is not applying yesterday's illusions to today's problems. As somebody said to me while I was studying for my degree in psychology in Chicago years ago, "Frequently, in the life of a priest, fifty years' experience is one year's experience repeated fifty times." You get the same solutions to fall back on: This is the way to deal with the alcoholic; this is the way to deal with priests; this is the way to deal with sisters; this is the way to deal with a divorcée. But that isn't wisdom. Wisdom is to be sensitive to *this* situation, to *this* person, uninfluenced by any carryover from the past, without residue from the experience of the past. This is quite unlike what most people are accustomed to thinking. I would add another sentence to the ones I've read: "If the heart is unobstructed, the result is love." I've been talking a great deal about love these days even though I told you there's nothing that can be said, really, about love. We can only speak of nonlove. We can only speak of addictions. But of love itself nothing may be said explicitly.

SAYING NOTHING
ABOUT LOVE

How would *I* describe love? I decided to give you one of the meditations I'm writing in a new book of mine. I'll read it to you slowly; you meditate on it as we go along, because I've got it put down in short form here so I can get it done in three or four minutes; otherwise it would take me half an hour. It's a comment on a gospel sentence. I had been thinking of another reflection, from Plato: "One cannot make a slave of a free person, for a free person is free even in prison." It's like another gospel sentence: "If a person makes you go one mile, go two." You may think you've made a slave out of me by putting a load on my back, but you haven't. If a person is trying to change external reality by being out of prison in order to be free, he is a prisoner indeed. Freedom lies not in external circumstances; freedom resides in the heart. When you have attained wisdom, who can enslave you? Anyhow, listen to the gospel sentence I had in mind earlier: "He sent the people away, and after doing that he went up to the mountain to pray alone. It grew late and he was there all by himself." *That's* what love is all about. Has it ever occurred to you that you can only love when you are alone? What does it mean to love? It means to see a person, a situation, a thing as it really is, not as you imagine it to be. And to give it the response it deserves. You can hardly be said to love what you do not even see. And what prevents us from seeing? Our conditioning. Our concepts, our categories, our prejudices, our projections, the labels that we have drawn from our cultures and our past experiences. Seeing is the most arduous thing that a human can undertake, for it calls for a disciplined, alert mind. But most people would much rather lapse into mental laziness than take the trouble to see each person, each thing in its present moment of freshness.

❦
LOSING CONTROL

If you wish to understand control, think of a little child that is given a taste for drugs. As the drugs penetrate the body of the child, it becomes addicted; its whole being cries out for the drug. To be without the drug is so unbearable a torment that it seems preferable to die. Think of that image —the body has gotten addicted to the drug. Now this is exactly what your society did to you when you were born. You were not allowed to enjoy the solid, nutritious food of life—namely, work, play, fun, laughter, the company of people, the pleasures of the senses and the mind. You were given a taste for the drug called approval, appreciation, attention.

I'm going to quote a great man here, a man named A. S. Neill. He is the author of *Summerhill*. Neill says that the sign of a sick child is that he is always hovering around his parents; he is interested in *persons*. The healthy child has no interest in persons, he is interested in *things*. When a child is sure of his mother's love, he forgets his mother; he goes out to explore the world; he is curious. He looks for a frog to put in his mouth—that kind of thing. When a child is hovering around his mother, it's a bad sign; he's insecure. Maybe his mother has been trying to suck love *out* of him, not give him all the freedom and assurance he wants. His mother's always been threatening in many subtle ways to abandon him.

So we were given a taste of various drug addictions: approval, attention, success, making it to the top, prestige, getting your name in the paper, power, being the boss. We were given a taste of things like being the captain of the team, leading the band, etc. Having a taste for these drugs, we became addicted and began to dread losing them. Recall the lack of control you felt, the terror at the prospect of failure or of making mistakes, at the prospect of criticism by others. So you became cravenly dependent on others and you lost your freedom. Others now have the power to make you happy or miserable. You crave your drugs, but as much as you hate the suffering that this involves, you find yourself completely helpless. There is never a minute when, consciously or unconsciously, you are not aware of or attuned to the reactions of others, marching to the beat of their drums. A nice definition of an awakened person: a person who no longer marches to the drums of society, a person who dances to the tune of the music that springs up from within. When you are ignored or disapproved of, you experience a loneliness so unbearable that you crawl back to people and beg for the comforting drug called support and encouragement, reassurance. To live with people in this state involves a never-ending tension. "Hell is other people," said

Sartre. How true. When you are in this state of dependency, you always have to be on your best behavior; you can never let your hair down; you've got to live up to expectations. To be with people is to live in tension. To be without them brings the agony of loneliness, because you miss them. You have lost your capacity to see them exactly as they are and to respond to them accurately, because your perception of them is clouded by the need to get your drugs. You see them insofar as they are a support for getting your drug or a threat to have your drug removed. You're always looking at people, consciously or unconsciously, through these eyes. Will I get what I want from them, will I not get what I want from them? And if they can neither support nor threaten my drug, I'm not interested in them. That's a horrible thing to say, but I wonder if there's anyone here of whom this cannot be said.

❧
LISTENING TO LIFE

Now, you need awareness and you need nourishment. You need good, healthy nourishment. Learn to enjoy the solid food of life. Good food, good wine, good water. Taste them. Lose your mind and come to your senses. That's good, healthy nourishment. The pleasures of the senses and the pleasures of the mind. Good reading, when you enjoy a good book. Or a really good discussion, or thinking. It's marvelous. Unfortunately, people have gone crazy, and they're getting more and more addicted because they do not know how to enjoy the lovely things of life. So they're going in for greater and greater artificial stimulants.

In the 1970s, President Carter appealed to the American people to go in for austerity. I thought to myself: He shouldn't tell them to be austere, he should really tell them to enjoy things. Most of them have lost their capacity for enjoyment. I really believe that most people in affluent countries have lost that capacity. They've got to have more and more expensive gadgets; they can't enjoy the simple things of life. Then I walk into places where they have all the most marvelous music, and you get these records at a discount, they're all stacked up, but I never hear anybody listening to them—no time, no time, no time. They're guilty, no time to enjoy life. They're overworked, go, go, go. If you really enjoy life and the simple pleasures of the senses, you'd be amazed. You'd develop that extraordinary discipline of the animal. An animal will never overeat. Left in its natural habitat, it will never be overweight. It will never drink or eat anything that is not good for its health. You never find an animal smoking. It always exercises as much as it needs—watch your cat after it's had its breakfast, look how it relaxes. And see how it springs into action, look at the suppleness of its limbs and the aliveness of its body. We've lost that. We're lost in our minds, in our ideas and ideals and so on, and its always go, go, go. And we've got an inner self-conflict which animals don't have. And we're always condemning ourselves and making ourselves feel guilty. You know what I'm talking about. I could have said of myself what one Jesuit friend said to me some years ago: Take that plate of sweets away, because in front of a plate of sweets or chocolates, I lose my freedom. That was true of me, too; I lost my freedom in front of all kinds of things, but no more! I'm satisfied with very little and I enjoy it intensely. When you have enjoyed something intensely, you need very little. It's like people who are busy planning their vacation; they spend months planning it, and they get to the spot, and they're all anxious about their reservations for flying back. But they're taking pictures alright, and later they'll show you pictures in an album, of places they never saw but only photographed. That's a symbol of modern life. I cannot warn you enough about this kind of asceticism. Slow down and taste and smell and hear, and let your senses come alive. If you want a royal road to mysticism, sit down quietly and listen to all the sounds around you. You do not focus on any one sound; you try to hear them all. Oh, you'll see the miracles that happen to you when your senses come unclogged. That is extremely important for the process of change.

THE END OF ANALYSIS

I want to give you a taste of the difference between analysis and awareness, or information on the one hand and insight on the other. Information is not insight, analysis is not awareness, knowledge is not awareness. Suppose I walked in here with a snake crawling up my arm, and I said to you, "Do you see the snake crawling up my arm? I've just checked in an encyclopedia before coming to this session and I found out that this snake is known as a Russell's viper. If it bit me, I would die inside half a minute. Would you kindly suggest ways and means by which I could get rid of this creature that is crawling up my arm?" Who talks like this? I have information, but I've got no awareness.

Or say I'm destroying myself with alcohol. "Kindly describe ways and means by which I could get rid of this addiction." A person who would say that has no awareness. He knows he's destroying himself, but he is not aware of it. If he were aware of it, the addiction would drop that minute. If I were aware of what the snake was, I wouldn't brush it off my arm; *it would get brushed off through me*. That's what I'm talking about, that's the change I'm talking about. You don't change yourself; it's not *me* changing *me*. Change takes place *through* you, in you. That's about the most adequate way I can express it. You see change take place in you, through you; in your awareness, it happens. *You* don't do it. When you're doing it, it's a bad sign; it won't last. And if it does last, God have mercy on the people you're living with, because you're going to be very rigid. People who are converted on the basis of self-hatred and self-dissatisfaction are impossible to live with. Somebody said, "If you want to be a martyr, marry a saint." But in awareness, you keep your softness, your subtleness, your gentleness, your openness, your flexibility, and you don't push, change occurs.

I remember a priest in Chicago when I was studying

psychology there telling us, "You know, I had all the information I needed; I knew that alcohol was killing me, and, believe me, nothing changes an alcoholic—not even the love of his wife or his kids. He does love them but it doesn't change him. I discovered one thing that changed me. I was lying in a gutter one day under a slight drizzle. I opened my eyes and I saw that this was killing me. I saw it and I never had the desire to touch a drop after that. As a matter of fact, I've even drunk a bit since then, but never enough to damage me. I couldn't do it and still cannot do it." That's what I'm talking about: awareness. Not information, but awareness.

A friend of mine who was given to excessive smoking said, "You know, there are all kinds of jokes about smoking. They tell us that tobacco kills people, but look at the ancient Egyptians; they're all dead and none of them smoked." Well, one day he was having trouble with his lungs, so he went to our cancer research institute in Bombay. The doctor said, "Father, you've got two patches on your lungs. It could be cancer, so you'll have to come back next month." He never touched another cigarette after that. Before, he *knew* it would kill him; now, he was *aware* it could kill him. That's the difference.

The founder of my religious order, St. Ignatius, has a nice expression for that. He calls it tasting and feeling the truth—not knowing it, but tasting and feeling it, getting a feel for it. When you get a feel for it you change. When you know it in your head, you don't.

🍎
DEAD AHEAD

I've often said to people that the way to really live is to die. The passport to living is to imagine yourself in your grave. Imagine that you're lying in your coffin. Any posture you like. In India we put them in cross-legged. Sometimes they're carried that way to the burning ground. Sometimes, though, they're lying flat. So imagine you're lying flat and you're dead. Now look at your problems from that viewpoint. Changes everything, doesn't it?

What a lovely, lovely meditation. Do it every day if you have the time. It's unbelievable, but you'll come alive. I have a meditation about that in a book of mine, *Wellsprings*. You see the body decomposing, then bones, then dust. Every time I talk about this, people say, "How disgusting!" But what's so disgusting about it? It's reality, for heaven's sake. But many of you don't want to see reality. You don't want to think of death. People don't live, most of you, you don't live, you're just keeping the body alive. That's not life. You're not living until it doesn't matter a tinker's damn to you whether you live or die. At that point you live. When you're ready to lose your life, you live it. But if you're protecting your life, you're dead. If you're sitting up there in the attic and I say to you, "Come on down!" and you say, "Oh no, I've read about people going down stairs. They slip and they break their necks; it's too dangerous." Or I can't get you to cross the street because you say, "You know how many people get run over when they cross the street?" If I can't get you to cross a street, how can I get you to cross a continent? And if I can't get you to peep out of

your little narrow beliefs and convictions and look at another world, you're dead, you're completely dead; life has
passed you by. You're sitting in your little prison, where
you're frightened; you're going to lose your God, your
religion, your friends, all kinds of things. Life is for the
gambler, it really is. That's what Jesus was saying. Are you
ready to risk it? Do you know when you're ready to risk it?
When you've discovered that, when you know that this
thing that people call life is not really life. People mistak-
enly think that living is keeping the body alive. So love the
thought of death, love it. Go back to it again and again.
Think of the loveliness of that corpse, of that skeleton, of
those bones crumbling till there's only a handful of dust.
From there on, what a relief, what a relief. Some of you
probably don't know what I'm talking about at this point;
you're too frightened to think of it. But it's such a relief
when you can look back on life from that perspective.

Or visit a graveyard. It's an enormously purifying and
beautiful experience. You look at this name and you say,
"Gee, he lived so many years ago, two centuries ago; he
must have had all the problems that I have, must have had
lots of sleepless nights. How crazy, we live for such a short
time. An Italian poet said, "We live in a flash of light;
evening comes and it is night forever." It's only a flash and
we waste it. We waste it with our anxiety, our worries, our
concerns, our burdens. Now, as you make that meditation,
you can just end up with information; but you may end up
with awareness. And in that moment of awareness, you are

new. At least as long as it lasts. Then you'll know the difference between information and awareness.

An astronomer friend was recently telling me some of the fundamental things about astronomy. I did not know, until he told me, that when you see the sun, you're seeing it where it was eight and a half minutes ago, not where it is now. Because it takes a ray of the sun eight and a half minutes to get to us. So you're not seeing it where it is; it's now somewhere else. Stars, too, have been sending light to us for hundreds of thousands of years. So when we're looking at them, they may not be where we're seeing them; they may be somewhere else. He said that, if we imagine a galaxy, a whole universe, this earth of ours would be lost toward the tail end of the Milky Way; not even in the center. And every one of the stars is a sun and some suns are so big that they could contain the sun and the earth and the distance between them. At a conservative estimate, there are one hundred million galaxies! The universe, as we know it, is expanding at the rate of two million miles a second. I was fascinated listening to all of this, and when I came out of the restaurant where we were eating, I looked up there and I had a different feel, a different perspective on life. That's awareness. So you can pick all this up as cold fact (and that's information), or suddenly you get another perspective on life—what are we, what's this universe, what's human life? When you get that feel, that's what I mean when I speak of awareness.

THE LAND OF LOVE

If we really dropped illusions for what they can give us or deprive us of, we would be alert. The consequence of not doing this is terrifying and unescapable. We lose our capacity to love. If you wish to love, you must learn to see again. And if you wish to see, you must learn to give up your drug. It's as simple as that. Give up your dependency. Tear away the tentacles of society that have enveloped and suffocated your being. You must drop them. Externally, everything will go on as before, but though you will continue to be *in* the world, you will no longer be *of* it. In your heart, you will now be free at last, if utterly alone. Your dependence on your drug will die. You don't have to go to the desert; you're right in the middle of people; you're enjoying them immensely. But they no longer have the power to make you happy or miserable. That's what aloneness means. In this solitude your dependence dies. The capacity to love is born. One no longer sees others as means of satisfying one's addiction. Only someone who has attempted this knows the terrors of the process. It's like inviting yourself to die. It's like asking the poor drug addict to give up the only happiness he has ever known. How to replace it with the taste of bread and fruit and the clean taste of the morning air, the sweetness of the water of the mountain stream? While he is struggling with his withdrawal symptoms and the emptiness he experiences within himself now that his drug is gone, nothing can fill the emptiness except his drug. Can you imagine a life in which you refuse to enjoy or take pleasure in a single word of appreciation or to rest your head on anyone's shoulder for support? Think of a life in which you depend on no one emotionally, so that no one has the power to make you happy or miserable anymore. You refuse to *need* any particular person or to be special to anyone or to call anyone your own. The birds of the air have their nests and the foxes their holes, but you will have nowhere to rest your head in your journey through life. If you ever get to this state, you will at last know what it means to see with a vision that is clear and unclouded by fear or desire. Every word there is measured. *To see at last with a vision that is clear and unclouded by fear or desire.* You will know what it means to love. But to come to the land of love, you must pass through the pains of death, for to love persons means to die to the need for persons, and to be utterly alone.

How would you ever get there? By a ceaseless awareness, by the infinite patience and compassion you would have for a drug addict. By developing a taste for the good things in life to counter the craving for your drug. What good things? The love of work which you enjoy doing for the love of itself; the love of laughter and intimacy with people to whom you do not cling and on whom you do not depend emotionally but whose company you enjoy. It will also help if you take on activities that you can do with your *whole being,* activities that you so love to do that while you're engaged in them success, recognition, and approval simply do not mean a thing to you. It will help, too, if you return to nature. Send the crowds away, go up to the mountains, and silently commune with trees and flowers and animals and birds, with sea and clouds and sky and stars. I've told you what a spiritual exercise it is to gaze at things, to be aware of things around you. Hopefully, the words will drop, the concepts will drop, and you will see, you will make contact with reality. That is the cure for loneliness. Generally, we seek to cure our loneliness through emotional dependence on people, through gregariousness and noise. That is no cure. Get back to things, get back to nature, go up in the mountains. Then you will know that your heart has brought you to the vast desert of solitude, there is no one there at your side, absolutely no one.

At first this will seem unbearable. But it is only because you are unaccustomed to aloneness. If you manage to stay there for a while, the desert will suddenly blossom into love. Your heart will burst into song. And it will be springtime forever; the drug will be out; you're free. Then you will understand what freedom is, what love is, what happiness is, what reality is, what truth is, what God is. You will see, you will know beyond concepts and conditioning, addictions and attachments. Does that make sense?

Let me end this with a lovely story. There was a man who invented the art of making fire. He took his tools and went to a tribe in the north, where it was very cold, bitterly cold. He taught the people there to make fire. The people were very interested. He showed them the uses to which they could put fire—they could cook, could keep themselves warm, etc. They were so grateful that they had learned the art of making fire. But before they could express their gratitude to the man, he disappeared. He wasn't concerned with getting their recognition or gratitude; he was concerned about their well-being. He went to another tribe, where he again began to show them the value of his invention. People were interested there, too, a bit too interested for the peace of mind of their priests, who began to notice that this man was drawing crowds and they were losing their popularity. So they decided to do away with him. They poisoned him, crucified him, put it any way you like. But they were afraid now that the people might turn against them, so they were very wise, even wily. Do you know what they did? They had a portrait of the man made and mounted it on the main altar of the temple. The instruments for making fire were placed in front of the portrait, and the people were taught to revere the portrait and to pay reverence to the instruments of fire, which they dutifully did for centuries. The veneration and the worship went on, but there was no fire.

Where's the fire? Where's the love? Where's the drug uprooted from your system? Where's the freedom? This is what spirituality is all about. Tragically, we tend to lose sight of this, don't we? This is what Jesus Christ is all about. But we overemphasized the "Lord, Lord," didn't we? Where's the fire? And if worship isn't leading to the fire, if adoration isn't leading to love, if the liturgy isn't leading to a clearer perception of reality, if God isn't leading to life, of what use is religion except to create more division, more fanaticism, more antagonism? It is not from lack of religion in the ordinary sense of the word that the world is suffering, it is from lack of love, lack of awareness. And love is generated through awareness and through no other way, no other way. Understand the obstructions you are putting in the way of love, freedom, and happiness and they will drop. Turn on the light of awareness and the darkness will disappear. Happiness is not something you acquire; love is not something you produce; love is not something that you have; love is something that *has* you. You do not have the wind, the stars, and the rain. You don't possess these things; you surrender to them. And surrender occurs when you are aware of your illusions, when you are aware of your addictions, when you are aware of your desires and fears. As I told you earlier, first, psychological insight is a great help, not analysis, however; analysis is paralysis. Insight is not necessarily analysis. One of your great American therapists put it very well: "It's the 'Aha' experience that counts." Merely analyzing gives no help; it just gives information. But if you could produce the "Aha" experience, that's insight. That is change. Second, the understanding of your addiction is important. You need time. Alas, so much time that is given to worship and singing praise and singing songs could so fruitfully be employed in self-understanding. Community is not produced by joint liturgical celebrations. You know deep down in your heart, and so do I, that such celebrations only serve to paper over differences. Community is created by understanding the blocks that we put in the way of community, by understanding the conflicts that arise from our fears and our desires. At that point community arises. We must always beware of making worship just another distraction from the important business of living.

And living doesn't mean working in government, or being a big businessman, or performing great acts of charity. That isn't living. Living is to have dropped all the impediments and to live in the present moment with freshness. "The birds of the air . . . they neither toil nor spin"—that is living. I began by saying that people are asleep, dead. Dead people running governments, dead people running big business, dead people educating others; come alive! Worship must help this, or else it's useless. And increasingly—you know this and so do I—we're losing the youth everywhere. They hate us; they're not interested in having more fears and more guilts laid on them. They're not interested in more sermons and exhortations. But they are interested in learning about love. How can I be happy? How can I live? How can I taste these marvelous things that the mystics speak of? So that's the second thing—understanding. Third, don't identify. Somebody asked me as I was coming here today, "Do you ever feel low?" Boy, do I feel low every now and then. I get my attacks. But they don't last, they really don't. What do I do? First step: I don't identify. Here comes a low feeling. Instead of getting tense about it, instead of getting irritated with myself about it, I understand I'm feeling depressed, disappointed, or whatever. Second step: I admit the feeling is in me, not in the other person, e.g., in the person who didn't write me a letter, not in the exterior world; it's in me. Because as long as I think it's outside me, I feel justified in holding on to my feelings. I can't say everybody would feel this way; in fact, only idiotic people would feel this way, only sleeping people. Third step: I don't identify with the feeling. "I" is not that feeling. "I" am not lonely, "I" am not depressed, "I" am not disappointed. Disappointment is *there,* one watches it. You'd be amazed how quickly it glides away. Anything you're aware of keeps changing; clouds keep moving. As you do this, you also get all kinds of insights into why clouds were coming in the first place.

I've got a lovely quote here, a few sentences that I would write in gold. I picked them up from A. S. Neill's book *Summerhill.* I must give you the background. You probably know that Neill was in education for forty years. He developed a kind of maverick school. He took in boys and girls and just let them be free. You want to learn to read and write, fine; you don't want to learn to read and write, fine. You can do anything you want with your life, provided you don't interfere with the freedom of someone else. Don't interfere with someone else's freedom; otherwise you're free. He says that the worst ones came to him from convent school. This was in the old days, of course. He said it took them about six months to get over all the anger and the resentment that they had repressed. They'd be rebelling for six months, fighting the system. The worst was a girl who would take a bicycle and ride into town, avoiding class, avoiding school, avoiding everything. But once they got over their rebellion, everybody wanted to learn; they even began protesting, "Why don't we have class today?" But they would only take what they were interested in. They'd be transformed. In the beginning parents were frightened to send their children to this school; they said, "How can you educate them if you don't discipline them? You've got to teach them, guide them." What was the secret of Neill's success? He'd get the worst children, the ones everybody else had despaired of, and within six months they'd all be transformed. Listen to what he said—extraordinary words, holy words. "Every child has a god in him. Our attempts to mold the child will turn the god into a devil. Children come to my school, little devils, hating the world, destructive, unmannerly, lying, thieving, bad-tempered. In six months they are happy, healthy children who do no evil." These are amazing words coming from a man whose school in Britain is regularly inspected by people from the Ministry of Education, by any headmaster or headmistress or anyone who would care to go there. Amazing. It was his charism. You don't do this kind of thing from a blueprint; you've got to be a special kind of person. In some of his lectures to headmasters and headmistresses he says, "Come to Summerhill and you'll find that all the fruit trees are laden with fruit; nobody's taking the fruits off the trees; there's no desire to attack authority; they're well fed and there's no resentment and anger. Come to Summerhill and you'll never find a handicapped child with a nickname (you know how cruel kids can be when someone stammers). You'll never find anyone needling a stammerer, never. There's no violence in those children, because no one is practicing violence on them, that's why." Listen to these words of revelation, sacred words. We have people in the world like this. No matter what scholars and priests and theologians tell you, there are and have been people who have no quarrels, no jealousies, no conflicts, no wars, no enmities, none! They exist in my country, or, sad to say, they existed until relatively recently. I've had Jesuit friends go out to live and work among people who, they assured me, were incapable of stealing or lying. One Sister said to me that when she went to the northeast of India to work among some tribes there, the people would lock up nothing. Nothing was ever stolen and they never told lies—until the Indian government and missionaries showed up.

Every child has a god in him; our attempts to mold the child will turn the god into a devil.

There's a lovely Italian film directed by Federico Fellini, *8½*. In one scene there's a Christian Brother going out on a picnic or excursion with a group of eight- to ten-year-old boys. They're on a beach, moving right on ahead while the Brother brings up the rear with three or four of them around him. They come across an older woman who's a whore, and they say to her, "Hi," and she says, "Hi." And they say, "Who are you?" And she says, "I'm a prostitute." They don't know what that is but they pretend to. One of the boys, who seems a bit more knowing than the others, says, "A prostitute is a woman who does certain things if you pay her." They ask, "Would she do those things if we paid her?" "Why not?" the answer came. So they take up a collection and give her the money, saying, "Would you do certain things now that we've given you the money?" She answers, "Sure, kids, what do you want me to do?" The only thing that occurs to the kids is for her to take her clothes off. So she does. Well, they look at her; they've never seen a woman naked before. They don't know what else to do, so they say, "Would you dance?" She says, "Sure." So they all gather round singing and clapping; the whore is moving her behind and they're enjoying themselves immensely. The Brother sees all this. He runs down the beach and yells at the woman. He gets her to put her clothes on, and the narrator says, "At that moment, the children were spoiled; until then they were innocent, beautiful."

This is not an unusual problem. I know a rather conservative missionary in India, a Jesuit. He came to a workshop of mine. As I developed this theme over two days, he suffered. He came to me the second night and said, "Tony, I can't explain to you how much I'm suffering listening to you." I said, "Why, Stan?" He said, "You're reviving within me a question that I suppressed for twenty-five years, a horrible question. Again and again I asked myself: Have I not spoiled my people by making them Christian?" This Jesuit was not one of your liberals, he was an orthodox, devout, pious, conservative man. But he felt he spoiled a happy, loving, simple, guileless people by making them Christian.

American missionaries who went to the South Sea Islands with their wives were horrified to see women coming barebreasted to church. The wives insisted that the women should be more decently dressed. So the missionaries gave them shirts to wear. The following Sunday the women came wearing their shirts but with two big holes cut out for comfort, for ventilation. They were right; the missionaries were wrong.

Now . . . back to Neill. He says, "And I am no genius, I am merely a man who refuses to guide the steps of children." But what, then, of original sin? Neill says that every child has a god in him; our attempts to mold him will turn the god into a devil. He lets children form their own values, and the values are invariably good and social. Can you believe that? When a child feels loved (which means: when a child feels you're on his side), he's O.K. The child doesn't experience violence anymore. No fear, so no violence. The child begins to treat others the way he has been treated. You've got to read that book. It's a holy book, it really is. Read it; it revolutionized my life and my dealings with people. I began to see miracles. I began to see the self-dissatisfaction that had been ingrained in me, the competition, the comparisons, the that's-not-good-enough, etc. You might object that if they hadn't pushed me, I wouldn't have become what I am. Did I need all that pushing? And anyway, who wants to be what I am? I want to be happy, I want to be holy, I want to be loving, I want to be at peace, I want to be free, I want to be human.

Do you know where wars come from? They come from projecting outside of us the conflict that is inside. Show me an individual in whom there is no inner self-conflict and I'll show you an individual in whom there is no violence. There will be effective, even hard, action in him, but no hatred. When he acts, he acts as a surgeon acts; when he acts, he acts as a loving teacher acts with mentally retarded children. You don't blame them, you understand; but you swing into action. On the other hand, when you swing into action with your own hatred and your own violence unaddressed, you've compounded the error. You've tried to put fire out with more fire. You've tried to deal with a flood by adding water to it. I repeat what Neill said: "Every child has a god in him. Our attempts to mold the child will turn the god into a devil. Children come to my school, little devils, hating the world, destructive, unmannerly, lying, thieving, bad-tempered. In six months they are happy, healthy children who do no evil. And I am no genius, I am merely a man who refuses to guide the steps of children. I let them form their own values and the values are invariably good and social. The religion that makes people good makes people bad, but the religion known as freedom makes all people good, for it destroys the inner conflict [I've added the word "inner"] that makes people devils."

Neill also says, "The first thing I do when a child comes to Summerhill is destroy its conscience." I assume you know what he's talking about, because I know what he's talking about. You don't need conscience when you have consciousness; you don't need conscience when you have sensitivity. You're not violent, you're not fearful. You probably think this is an unattainable ideal. Well, read that book. I have run into individuals, here and there, who suddenly stumble upon this truth: The root of evil is within you. As you begin to understand this, you stop making demands on yourself, you stop having expectations of yourself, you stop pushing yourself and you understand. Nourish yourself on wholesome food, good wholesome food. I'm not talking about actual food, I'm talking about sunsets, about nature, about a good movie, about a good book, about enjoyable work, about good company, and hopefully you will break your addictions to those other feelings.

What kind of feeling comes upon you when you're in touch with nature, or when you're absorbed in work that you love? Or when you're really conversing with someone whose company you enjoy in openness and intimacy without clinging? What kind of feelings do you have? Compare those feelings with the feelings you have when you win an argument, or when you win a race, or when you become popular, or when everybody's applauding you. The latter feelings I call worldly feelings; the former feelings I call soul feelings. Lots of people gain the world and lose their soul. Lots of people live empty, soulless lives because they're feeding themselves on popularity, appreciation, and praise, on "I'm O.K., you're O.K.," look at me, attend to me, support me, value me, on being the boss, on having power, on winning the race. Do you feed yourself on that? If you do, you're dead. You've lost your soul. Feed yourself on other, more nourishing material. Then you'll see the transformation. I've given you a whole program for life, haven't I?

ANTHONY DE MELLO, S.J., was the director of the Sadhana Institute of Pastoral Counseling in Poona, India. A member of the Jesuit province of Bombay, he was widely known in English- and Spanish-speaking countries for his retreats, workshops, seminars on prayer, and therapy courses—work which he was involved in for over eighteen years around the world. Though he died suddenly in 1987, he leaves a rich legacy of spiritual teaching through his written and recorded words.

REV. J. FRANCIS STROUD, S.J., a Campus Minister at Fordham University in New York, is also the Executive Director of the De Mello Spirituality Center and worked closely with Anthony de Mello for eight years.